T0301196

2025

HOROSCOPE

Also by the author:

Capricorn
Aquarius
Pisces
Aries
Taurus
Gemini
Cancer
Leo
Virgo
Libra
Scorpio
Sagittarius

SALLY KIRKMAN

2025

HOROSCOPE

First published in Great Britain in 2024 by Yellow Kite
An imprint of Hodder & Stoughton Limited
An Hachette UK company

1

A CIP catalogue record for this title is available from the British Library

Hardback ISBN 978 1 399 73171 3
ebook ISBN 978 1 399 73172 0

Typeset in Apollo MT Std by
Palimpsest Book Production Ltd, Falkirk, Stirlingshire

Printed and bound in Great Britain by Clays Ltd, Elcograf S.p.A.

Hodder & Stoughton policy is to use papers that are natural, renewable
and recyclable products and made from wood grown in sustainable forests.
The logging and manufacturing processes are expected to conform
to the environmental regulations of the country of origin.

Hodder & Stoughton Limited
Carmelite House
50 Victoria Embankment
London EC4Y 0DZ

www.yellowkitebooks.co.uk

INTRODUCTION

Astrology is an ancient art that can help us find meaning and reassurance in our busy and technological modern world.

Before the internet, before computers, before books – even before a shared language – people were fascinated by the movement of the stars and planets, creating stories and myths around them. They observed the cycles of nature and the movement of the Sun, Moon, stars and planets. In ancient times, people were closely connected with the Earth and the celestial realm. The saying 'as above, so below' was a popular phrase that expressed the idea that the movement of the planets and stars mirrored life on earth and human affairs.

We are living in a different world now, one in which scientific truth is paramount, yet many people are still seeking meaning. Our lives have been dominated by the power of the internet, seemingly giving us access to all the information we could ever need and allowing us to make endless connections in our lives. The consequence is that we have forgotten our connection with the Earth and the universe. This often leads to a sense of being disconnected from the natural world because we have switched off from our instinctual self and our inner knowingness.

**When you listen to the universe,
it's always talking to you.**

The calling for something more, the sense that there's a profound truth beyond the objective and scientific that reconnects us with ancient knowledge and wisdom, is what leads people to astrology and similar disciplines that embrace a universal truth, an intuitive knowingness. Astrology means 'language of the stars' and people today are rediscovering the relevance and wisdom of this ancient art.

When you learn how to tune in and listen, you will see that our world is primed with signs and synchronicities. The more you connect to the natural cycles of life, the more you feel in flow and guided by the rhythms of the universe. This is one of astrology's core benefits, helping you connect on a deeper level to yourself and what lies beyond, in an increasingly unpredictable world.

**The stars are within you
and you are in the stars.**

HOW TO USE THIS BOOK

The first part of *2025 Horoscope* includes a brief introduction to some astrology concepts to be aware of, that will help you to understand what to expect for your sign for 2025, in case you are not already familiar.

The next section is an overview of the astrology and the major planetary phenomena taking place throughout the year – a guide to what's happening when. The timing of astrology can be helpful in pinpointing those times in the year when it would be wise to retreat or go slow, as well as when to embrace life to the full and adopt a risk-taking attitude that will reap rewards. This enables you to be in tune with life and in flow, instead of feeling blocked or off track. Having a bigger picture of the seven traditional planetary bodies (the Sun, the Moon, Mercury, Venus, Mars, Jupiter and Saturn) and the three modern planets (Uranus, Neptune and Pluto) add information and fine-tuning to your year ahead. Knowing about the eclipses and the retrograde phases of the planets is vital in working with the timing of astrology.

All planets have repeating patterns and examining their cycles can help you understand your past and – crucially – what's happening now and what's to come. You can learn from these repeat patterns, know better how to avoid mistakes and be successful in your future goals.

The final – and most important – part of the book reveals your individual horoscope for the coming year based on your Sun (or star) sign. Each of the twelve signs includes key information about your sign, top tips for the year ahead, information about your ruling planet and a list of lucky dates, as well as key information on subjects from love and money to communication, health and well-being. All this can help you to determine the areas of your life where opportunities abound and those areas where it's wise to be cautious.

Being in tune with astrology is like having a superpower to

see your life from a new and different perspective. So use your *2025 Horoscope* as a guide to make the most of your year and to help increase your understanding and insight of yourself. It can help you discover the opportunities available to you and gain knowledge that you can put to good use in the year ahead.

All the dates in the book are correct for GMT time zone. Depending where you live in the world, the planetary event may fall late the day before or early the next day. It's great to work with the dates of cosmic events so you can make plans and use the astrology to your advantage. Although it's worth noting that planetary events don't always coincide precisely with events in your life to the moment. Sometimes, things happen the day before or the day after that resonate with what's happening in the planets. For example, you often feel Full Moon energy a couple of days before and you can set your intentions on the New Moon in the couple of days after the cosmic event.

ABOUT SALLY

Despite having thirty-five years of experience working as an astrologer, I am still continually delighted and amazed by the language of the stars. If you have come to me for an astrology reading or listen into my popular monthly astrology podcast, you'll know that my approach to astrology is direct, honest and real. This is my goal in writing your horoscopes for the year ahead. I like to bring astrology to life for you, to speak its language in a down-to-earth voice. My aim is to make a complex art easy for you to understand, so you know what's happening and what it means for you.

Additionally, I want you to reconnect with the planets and stars in the sky. To know when there's a New Moon and Full

Moon and how to work with them; to revel in the constancy and beauty of the Sun rising and setting. Nature and the universe is all around you and being in tune with the cosmos adds depth and meaning to your life.

Astrology is a powerful tool that enables you to make guided decisions in your life. It can reassure you when times are tough and help you make the most of your potential. A little knowledge and understanding means you can use the timing of astrology to your advantage. When you're in flow, synchronicities happen to you more often and you feel guided by something deeper than yourself.

ASTROLOGY
INFORMATION

STAR SIGNS

EQUINOX
Aries (21 March – 19 April)
Taurus (20 April – 20 May)
Gemini (21 May – 20 June)

SOLSTICE
Cancer (21 June – 22 July)
Leo (23 July – 22 August)
Virgo (23 August – 22 September)

EQUINOX
Libra (23 September – 23 October)
Scorpio (24 October – 22 November)
Sagittarius (23 November – 21 December)

SOLSTICE
Capricorn (22 December – 20 January)
Aquarius (21 January – 18 February)
Pisces (19 February – 20 March)

Note that the day/time the Sun enters each star sign changes slightly each year (within twenty-four hours). This means you don't know for sure what Sun sign you are if you're born on the cusp. If your birthday falls on the day either side of the Sun switching signs, you need to consult with an astrologer or draw up your birth chart, including your date, time and place of birth to find out where the Sun was when you were born. You can find this information on my website: sallykirkman.com.

THE PLANETS

Your horoscope is based on solar houses – i.e. it's the movement of the Sun through the zodiac which reveals what areas of your life are under the cosmic spotlight. However, if you've had an astrology reading or you've seen the map of the heavens for the time you were born, you will be aware that you are more than your Sun sign.

The Sun is the most important star in the sky because all the planets revolve around it. Yet, it's only one influence. In your horoscope, you'll see that all the planets are used to determine your fate. Here's a quick guide to what each planet represents in astrology.

THE SUN

The Sun represents your essence, your identity, who you are becoming. It's you as an adult, your public persona and the way you engage with the world. The Sun rules the light of the day and represents your father.

THE MOON

The Moon represents your needs, your inner self, what comforts you. It's you as a child, your private persona and where you seek security in your life. The Moon rules the dark of the night and represents your mother.

MERCURY

Mercury is the planet of communication, the messenger in mythology. It's the planet linked to the mind and tells you about the way you learn and your communication style.

VENUS

Venus is the goddess of love and tells you about the way you relate. It reveals what you want when it comes to love, what gives you pleasure, your values, what you desire. Venus rules women, money, art and beauty.

MARS

Mars is the god of war and tells you about your drive and ambition. It reveals the way you do business, your physical strength, what angers you and where your passions lie. Mars rules men, athleticism, sex and the libido.

JUPITER

Jupiter is the biggest and best planet in astrology. It tells you where you find good fortune and opportunity. Jupiter represents truth and justice, foreign connections, higher education, philosophy and religion. Wherever you find Jupiter in your horoscope, this is where you can pursue meaning and purpose and expand your life.

SATURN

Saturn is the outermost traditional planet and it's linked to endings and boundaries. It can be a heavy influence and reveals where you may encounter authority, limitations or hardship. Wherever you find Saturn in your horoscope, you may need to work hard or take things seriously. It can also lend you self-discipline and resilience.

URANUS

Uranus was discovered in 1781. It's the planet of change, revolution and innovation. The key psychological term is to 'dissociate'. Uranus's nature is future-oriented, impulsive and radical. Uranus is the awakener.

NEPTUNE

Neptune was discovered in 1846. It's the planet of dreams, fantasy and the imagination. The key psychological term is to 'dissolve'. Neptune's nature is seductive, empathic and blissful. Neptune is a creative or spiritual influence.

PLUTO

Pluto was discovered in 1930. It's the planet of power, transformation and control. The key psychological term is to 'destroy'. Pluto's nature is obsessive, intense and all-consuming. Pluto takes you on a journey into the underworld.

THE PLANETARY ASPECTS

Aspects are connections formed between planets depending where they are in the zodiac. The major planetary aspects are conjunction, sextile, square, trine and opposition.

Conjunction is a powerhouse aspect when two planets sit side by side, next to one another in the zodiac.

Sextile is an easy aspect when two planets are two signs apart, i.e. 60 degrees apart.

Square is a clashing or conflict aspect when two planets are square one another, i.e. 90 degrees apart.

Trine is a flowing aspect, when two planets are in a star sign of the same element, i.e. 120 degrees apart.

Opposition is when two planets are in opposite star signs, i.e. 180 degrees apart.

THE SYMMETRY
OF ASTROLOGY

There is a beautiful symmetry to the zodiac (see horoscope wheel, page xi). There are twelve zodiac signs, which can be divided into two sets of 'introvert' and 'extrovert' signs, four elements (fire, earth, air, water), three modes (cardinal, fixed, mutable) and six pairs of opposite star signs.

One of the attributes of astrology is in bringing opposites together, showing how they complement each other and work together, and, in so doing, restore unity. The horoscope wheel represents the cyclical nature of life.

ELEMENTS

There are four elements in astrology and three star signs allocated to each. The elements are:

1. Fire – Aries, Leo, Sagittarius
2. Earth – Taurus, Virgo, Capricorn

3. Air – Gemini, Libra, Aquarius
4. Water – Cancer, Scorpio, Pisces

This is what each element represents:

Fire – blazes bright. Fire types are inspirational, motivational and adventurous. They love starting things and having fun.

Earth – grounding and solid. Earth rules money, security and practicality. Earth represents the physical body and favours slow living.

Air – intangible, a vast entity. Air rules thinking, ideas, social interaction, debate and questioning. Air represents the air that we breathe and the airwaves.

Water – deep and healing. Water rules feelings, intuition, quietness, relating, giving and sharing. Water represents our emotions and our deeper connection with the flow of life.

MODES

There are three modes in astrology and four star signs allocated to each. The modes are:

1. Cardinal – Aries, Cancer, Libra, Capricorn
2. Fixed – Taurus, Leo, Scorpio, Aquarius
3. Mutable – Gemini, Virgo, Sagittarius, Pisces

What each mode represents:

Cardinal – The first group represents the leaders of the zodiac. These star signs love to take the initiative and be proactive. Some say they're controlling.

Fixed – The middle group holds fast and stands the middle ground. These star signs are stable and reliable. Some say they're stubborn.

Mutable – The last group goes with the flow and drifts through life. These star signs are flexible, adaptable and dual natured. Some say they're all over the place.

INTROVERT AND EXTROVERT STAR SIGNS/OPPOSITE STAR SIGNS

The introvert signs are the earth and water signs, and the extrovert signs are the fire and air signs. Both sets oppose each other across the zodiac.

The 'introvert' earth and water oppositions are:

Taurus – Scorpio
Cancer – Capricorn
Virgo – Pisces

The 'extrovert' air and fire oppositions are:

Aries – Libra
Gemini – Sagittarius
Leo – Aquarius

THE HOUSES

The houses (sectors) of the astrology wheel are an integral part of your horoscope. The symmetry that is inherent within astrology remains, as the wheel is divided into twelve equal sections, called 'houses'. Here's a list of the meanings of the twelve houses:

1. physical body, personal goals, image and profile
2. money, possessions, values, self-worth
3. communication, education, siblings, local neighbourhood
4. home, family, roots, the past, your legacy
5. creativity, romance, entertainment, children, luck
6. work, routine, health and lifestyle, service to others
7. relationships, the 'other', enemies, contracts
8. joint finances, other peoples' resources, all things hidden and taboo
9. travel, study, philosophy, legal affairs, publishing, religion
10. career, vocation, status and reputation
11. friends, groups, networks, your role within society
12. retreat, sacrifice, spirituality, inner self

WHAT TO EXPECT
IN 2025

Astrology works on both a personal and a collective level. As an introduction to your 2025 horoscopes, this section explores the wider significance of some of the most interesting movements of the planets in this period. This can tell us so much more about the world we live in. Whatever your personal situation moving into 2025, I'd like to wish you the best year possible, from the bottom of my heart. Thank you for joining me in caring about our amazing universe.

THE NEW AIR ERA

Life has changed profoundly since the start of this decade. Astrology has been an invaluable guide helping to navigate this unique time in history, bringing a fresh perspective. We're moving into a new age, a new era.

This is connected to the planetary cycle involving Jupiter and Saturn. In traditional astrology, before the discovery of the modern planets, Jupiter and Saturn were the most significant planets. They are still important and visible in the night sky. They meet once every twenty years and this encounter has always been an important symbol of the times.

For the last 200 years, the Jupiter–Saturn conjunctions have fallen primarily in the earth signs, Taurus, Virgo or Capricorn, which coincided with the Industrial Revolution, an era of production, manufacturing and excavating the material that forms our earth.

However, this is starting to change. The most recent Jupiter–Saturn conjunction took place in December 2020 in Aquarius, one of the air signs. This means we are at the beginning of a new 200-year cycle, during which the Jupiter–Saturn conjunctions will fall in the air signs, Aquarius, Gemini and Libra. The element air rules ideas, the sharing of information, networks, social connections, communication and technology.

Tim Berners-Lee invented the World Wide Web in 1989 during a rogue Jupiter–Saturn conjunction in Libra, an air sign. Since then, social media, mobile phones, global connections and online networks have exploded into our world.

The Covid/lockdown years gave us another clue about what this new air era will entail. In this period, the information superhighways took over from physical travel. Businesses swarmed online, relying on Zoom meetings and other virtual software. AI and automation are taking over tasks that have always been done by humans. Space too is opening up with more countries investing in space travel – the ultimate air adventure. Air represents the breath too, so maybe we will have to learn to live with new airborne viruses during the next chapter of our time on this earth.

The new air era promises changes to the collective at a political, social, humanitarian and environmental level. Some of the changes taking place may need to be radical. Everyone may have to become less self-oriented and more concerned about what's best for the whole.

This could be an exciting time for science, space travel, new-age thinkers, social activists, pioneering leaders, inventors, visionaries, rebels and innovators. Also, astrology and spirituality, community and the collective. There's going to be a significant shift towards new initiatives and ideas and the way people seek meaning in their lives.

Yet, in the new era, we mustn't forget what connects us as human beings, rather than what divides us or separates us. More people will be turning to the wider universe to find answers. It's a new paradigm, an era when new solutions, rules and visions are required. This is true both on a collective level and in your personal life.

THE MODERN PLANETS

This leads us into what's coming up in 2025. We are in a profoundly transitional phase, as the three modern planets — Uranus, Neptune and Pluto — are all changing, or have just changed, star sign. The modern planets are invisible to the naked eye. All were discovered over the last 250 years, starting with Uranus in 1781, then Neptune in 1846 and finally Pluto in 1930. Pluto was demoted from planetary status in 2006 but is still widely used in astrology and its power is evident. If you think that Uranus spends approximately seven years in one star sign, Neptune spends approximately twelve years in one star sign and Pluto spends approximately twenty years in one star sign, it's rare for them all to be on the move relatively close to one another.

The slowest-moving planet, Pluto, moved back and forth between earth sign Capricorn and air sign Aquarius in 2023 and 2024. Then, on 19 November 2024, Pluto took up residence in Aquarius where it will remain for the next twenty years.

And this year, Uranus moves into another air sign, Gemini. Plus, Neptune makes a major move as it leaves the last sign of the zodiac Pisces and enters the first sign of the zodiac Aries.

What's helpful moving forward is that positive connections between the planets in Aries, Gemini and Aquarius means that the modern planets will be working well together. This could mean that the new era is going to move ahead at a fast rate of knots, as new technologies and inventions come to the fore. What's important, however, with these major transitions of the planets, is that things don't have to happen overnight. This is a transitional phase and, when you look at back at times in history, it can take years for a new era or age to be formed.

In 2025, Uranus and Neptune both try out their respective new star signs, but the major shift comes next year. In 2025, Uranus will spend almost eight months in earth sign Taurus and Neptune spends five months in water sign Pisces. Taurus is linked to money, production, nature and the earth we stand on. Pisces is linked to water, spirituality, the collective unconscious and the sea. There's a flow between these two star signs, a helpful, easy connection. Therefore, we must continue to pay attention to our earth and our seas, the food we eat and the water we drink. It's not wise to throw the baby out with the bathwater. Instead, we must learn from our experiences and cherish what we have, before leaping into something new.

THE OUTER PLANETS

Jupiter and Saturn are both visible in the night sky. Of the seven traditional planets, they represent the boundaries of our existence. They are significant planets within astrology. Both are seen as leaders or rulers, in keeping with their mythological archetypes.

Jupiter spends approximately one year in each star sign, meaning that everyone gets a boost of Jupiter joy every twelve years. In 2025, Jupiter will be in air sign Gemini up until June, when it moves into water sign Cancer. Both star signs can expect some good fortune in the year ahead.

Saturn is the slower-moving of the two planets, taking between two to three years to move through each star sign. This year, Saturn is also on the move, leaving the last star sign of the zodiac, Pisces, and entering the first sign of the zodiac, Aries. This transition completes in 2026.

Saturn is moving closer to Neptune in the zodiac in 2025. This is important because there will be an epic Saturn–Neptune conjunction in Aries in February 2026. We may discover more about what this conjunction will mean this year, as both planets are side by side in Aries in June, July and August.

ECLIPSES: PORTALS OF CHANGE

It's usual to have four eclipses during one year and they come in pairs. Eclipses are game-changers, when the wheel of fortune turns and the roller-coaster of life speeds up.

There will be two New Moon solar eclipses, which are portents of new beginnings: one in Aries on 29 March and one in Virgo on 21 September. Plus, there are going to be two Full Moon lunar eclipses, which can work as portals of change. The first will be in Virgo on 14 March and the second in Pisces on 7 September.

This years' eclipses fall in the same star signs as last year.

The Aries/Libra eclipses are completing in March 2025, and the Virgo/Pisces eclipses began in September 2024 and will complete in February 2027. If you're an Aries, Libra, Virgo or Pisces, you're in the swirl of eclipse energy. Yet the eclipses will be important for everyone – how will depend on where they fall in your horoscope.

RETROGRADE PLANETS

Mercury retrograde has become mainstream news and is often referenced by the media. When retrograde, the planet gives the illusion of moving backwards through the zodiac.

The messenger planet orbits the Sun the fastest and is always close to the Sun in the zodiac. Its retrograde phases occur regularly, approximately three times a year for three weeks at a time.

Traditionally, Mercury retrograde is associated with communication chaos, as Mercury is the communication planet. You can schedule the Mercury retrograde phases into your diary. Ideally, it's not the time to launch something new. Instead, take your foot off the accelerator and slow things down.

The two other inner planets, Venus and Mars, also turn retrograde – Venus approximately once every eighteen months and Mars approximately once every two years. It's rare that both planets have retrograde phases in the same year but this is what's happening in 2025.

Action planet Mars is retrograde in January and February. And Venus will be retrograde in March and April. Therefore, trying to rush into 2025 may not be the right approach, especially in some key areas of life. Mars rules drive and ambition, while Venus is the goddess of love, linked to money, art and beauty. So you might be wise to review and reassess your situation in the first few months of the year.

COSMIC BLESSINGS

As the Sun and the faster-moving planets Mercury, Venus and Mars move through the zodiac, they make lucky connections with Jupiter. Anything that begins under a Jupiter transit promises success.

This year, the star signs Gemini and Cancer will benefit the most from Jupiter's blessings in June and August. Aquarius gets a shot of Jupiter luck at the start of Aquarius birthday season – January/February. Then it's Aries' turn to embrace Jupiter's joy at the start of April, May and June. Earth sign Virgo aligns with Jupiter in June, then again in September and October. Scorpio may have to wait a while for those cosmic blessings but they're in abundance in Scorpio season – October/November – and again in December.

≋

PLUTO IN AQUARIUS:

TECHNOLOGY AND SOCIETY

We've had two years already to experience Pluto's move into air sign Aquarius, as it has been journeying in and out of Aquarius in 2023 and 2024. When I first wrote about Pluto entering Aquarius in 2023, it seemed a fitting symbol to give the title 'Power to the People' to this planet/sign combination.

Aquarius represents the people, the collective and society. It's the star sign linked to groups and friendship, humanitarian, environmental and social causes. Therefore, Pluto in Aquarius could play out as 'power (Pluto) to the people (Aquarius)'. The year of 2024 was the biggest one for elections globally in history; a nod towards Pluto's power in the star sign of the collective.

PLUTO IN AQUARIUS

23 March to 11 June 2023

11 January to 2 September 2024

19 November 2024 to 2043/2044

Yet, a symbol doesn't mean just one thing and another major showing of Pluto's move into Aquarius is the emergence of artificial intelligence. AI has been around for years but, as Pluto geared up ready to make its first move into Aquarius at the start of 2023, Artificial Intelligence was big news.

We've seen the brilliance and usefulness of AI and we are becoming more aware of the dangers. If we give our power away to machines and robots, who's in control? Pluto themes are often about power and control and who or what's in charge. Plus, our very creativity and the areas of life that matter so deeply, like art, theatre, storytelling, fiction, poems, music, therapy and so on, are all potentially under threat from artificial intelligence.

Will we lose our ability to be creative if we resort to clicking a button and seeing what AI splurges out? Is it another way we will become more disconnected from the earth, the universe, from emotional connection, from people and the things in life that really matter?

It's wise not to go forward blindly. Pluto's realm is the under-world, dark and shady. There are dangers lurking, as we know from Pluto's journey through earth sign Capricorn, 2008 to 2024. Capricorn is the star sign linked to big business and the estab-lishment. While Pluto's one of the planets linked to wealth, especially money that's hidden. The planet of the underworld governs all things corrupt and dark.

Pluto's transit through Capricorn elevated the role of the 'plutocrat' and the billionaires. We have been bombarded with examples of power, status and entitlement in positions of authority and leadership. There was a power grab for money and wealth, creating a stronger divide between the rich and poor. So, what else can we expect from Pluto's journey through Aquarius?

The last time Pluto was in Aquarius was from 1777–1798. This was the period when Uranus, the planet linked to rebellion and revolution, was discovered in 1781. Uranus is the modern planet that rules Aquarius and these two planets, Uranus and Pluto, often work together to change society. Some major events during this period were the American War of Independence, the French Revolution and the first convicts being shipped from Britain to Australia. *A Vindication of the Rights of Woman* by Mary Wollstonecraft, a fierce advocate for women's rights, was published too. You can see by these few examples that this was a time of sweeping change and social reform. These themes may be reawakened or reinvented with Pluto moving through Uranus's star sign Aquarius once again.

Although, let's not forget that even though Aquarius is the star sign linked to equality, it's a fixed star sign – i.e. dogmatic and stubborn.

Taking an idealistic view of an equal society hasn't always played out well in the past around the world, but there's always hope for a new future and a new age opening up. So here's hoping that Pluto's journey through Aquarius helps to create a more equal society and brings about a redistribution of wealth. And that it will herald a time of leadership, with those in charge caring more for the people they are governing than lining their own pockets.

II

MULTICULTURALISM

Jupiter is the best planet in astrology and the biggest planet in the universe. Therefore, it's always important to note where Jupiter is in the zodiac because it's the planet associated with good fortune and opportunity.

In mythology, Jupiter was a sky god, linked to expansion, benevolence and protection. Jupiter represents travel, higher education, the law, truth and justice, wherever you seek meaning and purpose in life and the bigger picture. At its best, Jupiter's nature is jovial, fortunate and lucky. What begins under a Jupiter transit often promises success. Jupiter takes twelve years to circuit the zodiac bringing its blessings to each of the star signs in turn.

JUPITER GEMINI

25 May 2024 to 9 June 2025

In May 2024, Jupiter entered air sign Gemini where it will remain this year until 9 June. The last time Jupiter was in Gemini was 2012, the year of the Olympics in London. London is a Gemini city, so it's appropriate that this huge and influential planet Jupiter was in Gemini when the Olympics took place there. Jupiter rules foreign connections, and while in Gemini, we saw countries around the world come together in a big and very successful sporting event.

The fact that London is a Gemini city is fitting for a place that's a diverse melting pot of different people, cultures and boroughs. One of the most famous quotes about London – 'When a man is tired of London, he is tired of life' – by the eighteenth-century author Samuel Johnson picks up on the Gemini buzz.

Multiculturalism is a key theme for Jupiter in Gemini, the global planet in the star sign of communication and language. The world's population has exploded over recent years and the plight of refugees is ongoing. Immigration is a charged political topic and what's right and wrong often divides opinion. In this climate, it's worth bearing in mind that Geminis are communicators who thrive on variety and are always on the move. In fact, Gemini rules words, language, gossip, reading, writing, the media, education, transport, short trips, neighbours, siblings and twins – a diverse group. And this is where we get to the crux of Gemini because this star sign is nothing if not flexible.

Gemini's nature is curious and it's a star sign that loves variety in life. Yet, with a short attention span, Gemini is not known for focus and concentration. However, while Jupiter is in Gemini, this expands mental faculties and social interactions, opening up ways that we can learn bigger and better ways to take in knowledge and pass it on. Everyone's an expert at something and anyone can write reams at a touch of a button with AI in full flow.

Jupiter's not always comfortable in Gemini, though, as Jupiter favours the big vision while Gemini prefers to multi-task and diversify. Gemini gets easily distracted. Therefore, for many of us to a greater or lesser extent, it may be a challenge to manage your time well, while Jupiter's here. Life may feel like it's speeding up when Jupiter is speeding through this air sign, just as Gemini skims through life seeking new stimulation on a daily basis.

Jupiter in Gemini can be witty, quick, diverse and dexterous, yet it can be superficial and aimless too. Remember to stop at times and check in with the bigger purpose of what you're doing and where you're heading.

♋

FAMILY VALUES

On 9 June, the planet of opportunity, Jupiter, leaves air sign Gemini and moves into water sign Cancer, where it will remain until 30 June 2026.

One of Jupiter's archetypes in astrology is the Great Protector and Jupiter is a benevolent influence. Therefore, it's no surprise that Jupiter likes to be in the star sign Cancer, a kind and caring combination. Jupiter is said to be exalted in Cancer, which means it's comfortable here and can play to its strengths.

Cancer is the star sign ruled by the reflective Moon, a symbol of the mother, of nurturing and nourishment. It is the family star sign, favouring comfort, nesting and close bonds.

JUPITER CANCER

9 June 2025 to 30 June 2026

You may be drawn back to the place you grew up while Jupiter's in Cancer. Or perhaps you're reflecting where your home is or what home means to you. You might be concerned with protecting your own home and making sure you have a comfy nest for your children, your parents or the people closest to you.

Cancer can be a star sign that holds on to the memories of the past and favours traditional values. Therefore, you might take a trip down memory lane while Jupiter's in Cancer. It's an ideal time to gather the clans and prioritise your family or loved ones. This feeling may not be limited to your own family either, as Cancer can be a patriotic star sign. For example, the USA's star sign is Cancer – born on Independence Day, 4 July, it's a deeply patriotic country.

Nelson Mandela (18 July 1918) was born with the Sun in Cancer and he's often thought of as the father of South Africa. In fact many people called him 'Tata', a Xhosa word for father.

Angela Merkel (17 July 1954), who was the chancellor of Germany is a Sun Cancer. She was given the nickname *Mutti* by the German people, the German word for mother.

Jupiter's move through Cancer may bring a wave of patriotism, which is different, even the opposite, from Jupiter in Gemini's multicultural theme. Yet, still, ultimately Cancer is a compassionate and caring star sign. The water signs, like Cancer, are emotional and Cancer in particular is sentimental and nostalgic.

While Jupiter's moving through Cancer, you may appreciate more affection and hugs. Gather your loved ones around you, plant your garden, encourage flowers and love to grow and flourish.

Your **Jupiter Return** takes place every 12 years –
ages 12, 24, 36, 48, 60, 72, 84, etc. This is when
Jupiter returns to the place it was in the zodiac
when you were born. It is a time of opportunity,
expansion, freedom and adventure.

✠

SATURN IN PISCES:

REALITY MEETS FANTASY

Saturn is the planet which represents boundaries, whereas Pisces is the most boundless star sign. Saturn's domain is mountains and rocks and Pisces is all about the sea. This is an unusual planet/sign combination.

This year, Saturn will be in Pisces up until 25 May and again from 1 September onwards. Will this be a compassionate, kind and caring Saturn? Or will Saturn's realm of reality dissolve Pisces' realm of fantasy and dreams?

SATURN PISCES
7 March 2023 to 25 May 2025
1 September 2025 to 14 February 2026

At its best, Saturn in Pisces could see new rules and regulations put in place that will help clean up our seas and rivers. This is sorely needed here in the UK where sewage is constantly being pumped into our waters, creating a toxic mix for the living beings that reside in the waterways. And making it very unpleasant to swim in.

At a global level, we know that the sea is filled with plastic and other materials that are non-biodegradable. A positive showing of Saturn in Pisces are organisations set up to harness the power of our seas and clean up the oceans. Hopefully, this will continue in 2025 while there's a strong focus on the water (Pisces) and earth (Taurus) signs. Sustainability must become mainstream if we're to stop depleting and damaging the earth's natural resources.

Also, Pisces rules liquids, alcohol and drugs, altered states, the media, spirituality and the collective consciousness. There's already a rise in interest in the potential healing capacity of psychedelic drugs and cannabis oil, and this is set to continue and increase.

Shamanism is another showing of Saturn in Pisces, returning to ancient ways to live a life that's closer to spirit.

It would be wonderful to see more regulation in the media. Right now, politics is decided by the lure of money, the media and social media.

Pisces is a slippery star sign and its zodiac symbol is two fishes swimming in opposite directions. It's good to be aware that there can be a thin line between truth and lies when Pisces loses its way. There may be an abrupt end to conspiracy theories. Or, perhaps they become mainstream. We may see more evidence of extraterrestrial life. Or, an upsurge in teetotalism. It's hard to know anymore what's true and what isn't. Anything can be reimagined or recreated as the digital world and its technologies are infinite. The metaverse is a reality and artificial intelligence is reaching extraordinary levels, not all good.

We seem to be careering towards a new future, which will have its benefits as well as its disadvantages. Let's hope that Saturn in Pisces can work well to bring out the best of their opposing natures.

Your first **Saturn Return** – when Saturn is once more in exactly the same place it was when you were born – takes place age thirty, your astrological coming of age, symbolising maturity and adulthood. Your second Saturn Return takes place age sixty, the official age which we used to associate with becoming a pensioner (not that you're likely to receive your state pension at sixty now!). Your third Saturn Return takes place age 90. If you're still active, that's an achievement in itself.

H

NEPTUNE IN PISCES:

THE DREAMER

Neptune is co-ruler of the star sign Pisces. This is the planet of dreams and the imagination, romance and escapism, linked to Hollywood glamour, the movies and the fantasy realm. It's a mystical, magical and cosmic influence and pushes back the boundaries of possibility.

Neptune has been in Pisces since 2012 but this year, it starts to change star sign. Neptune will be in Pisces up until 30 March and again from 22 October onwards.

NEPTUNE PISCES

3 February 2012 to 30 March 2025

22 October 2025 to 26 January 2026

When you connect fully with Neptune in Pisces, you may want to sail away on the ocean, reconnect with your faith or find a place where you can embrace your spiritual nature. Neptune asks you to forgive yourself, make a sacrifice and care for all humanity. It's a cosmic reminder that we're all one.

When you tap into the full extent of Neptune's realm, you can shoot stardust into the cosmos and explore the outermost regions of our vast universe. Engage with Neptune to take you above and beyond what you do, what you think, your everyday encounters.

At its best, Neptune takes you on a magical mystery tour, whether you fall in love, seek devotion, find your muse, tap into your creative and spiritual source or devote your life to service. Wherever Pisces falls in your horoscope, you may want to lose yourself. Perhaps, you're drawn towards an artistic project, a musical journey or a poetic path. Consider what takes you out of yourself in a good way and when you feel at your most selfless.

There is a proviso, however, as Neptune's flip side is delusion, addiction, deception and betrayal. Ensure you embrace the right kind of escapism and stay connected and rooted in reality.

Neptune's orbit

The planet Neptune takes approximately 165 years to circuit the zodiac. Therefore, it's unlikely that any human being will ever experience their Neptune Return. Even the Neptune Half Return doesn't happen for all of us as you need to be in your eighties before the planet reaches the furthest point from where it was when you were born. I like to think of this half return as a time when you can escape into an eternal realm of spiritual bliss and transcendence.

♉

MERCHANT OF CHANGE

Uranus is the planet linked to innovation, technology, revolution and change. Uranus has been in earth sign Taurus consistently since 2019 and we already know a lot about its impact. This year, Uranus is in Taurus until 7 July and again from 8 November. It will leave Taurus and not return for eighty years in 2026.

URANUS TAURUS

15 May to 6 November 2018

6 March 2019 to 7 July 2025

8 November 2025 to 26 April 2026

Uranus is the change merchant and Taurus is the star sign linked to money, security, land, food, produce, nature, art, sex and fertility. Uranus in Taurus has been a wake-up call for what we're doing to our Earth and our resources. A cashless society fits Uranus in Taurus symbolism, as does a digital revolution. Plus, we're heading towards a global food crisis.

We must continue to use the best of Uranus in Taurus this year to find more innovative ventures that can protect our Earth. Extinction Rebellion is the global environmental movement that uses non-violent civil disobedience in an attempt to halt mass extinction and minimise the risk of social collapse.

The organisation was first established in May 2018. This was the month Uranus moved into Taurus for the first time in almost eighty years. Plus, Extinction Rebellion's two founders are both Sun Taurus. Therefore, you can see how closely Uranus's move through Taurus ties into activating the fight for our survival on this planet.

A key signature of Uranus's move through Taurus in 2024 was the farmers' protests. Uranus is a radical and a key signature of protests. Taurus represents the land we cultivate and live on.

Wherever you find Taurus in your horoscope, consider how you can be a rebel or a radical. Alternatively, notice whether you're resistant to change. Taurus is one of the fixed star signs. Therefore, it's been quite the ride for Taurus to have the planet of change Uranus bringing both upheaval and excitement.

Your Uranus Half Return

Uranus's erratic orbit means this takes place between ages thirty-nine and forty-three. Think 'life begins at forty'. It can coincide with a mid-life crisis or a *carpe diem* revelation – seize the day, life is short! Your Uranus Return takes place aged eighty-four, which is an ideal time to 'give the finger' to the establishment or screech towards death exclaiming, 'Wow! What a ride!'

♈

PRACTICAL IDEALISM

This year, both planets Saturn and Neptune change star sign as they grow closer together in the heavens. They leave behind the last sign of the zodiac, Pisces, and enter the first sign of the zodiac, Aries. We're moving into new territory.

Saturn will be in Aries from 25 May to 1 September and Neptune will be in Aries from 30 March to 22 October. Both planets will take up residence in Aries next year. For Saturn, this will be until April 2028, and for Neptune, it will be for a longer time, until 2038/2039.

SATURN ARIES

Saturn in Aries is an uncomfortable combination. Aries is a fire sign that likes to be impulsive, radical and independent. Whereas Saturn represents rules and laws; it's a slow and steady influence and favours patience over spontaneous impulses.

You might want to rise up against the system when Saturn's

in Aries. Yet doing your own thing (Aries) could get you into trouble with the authorities (Saturn).

At its best, this combination is strident, a blazing fury and headstrong. Be wary of starting something new, however, and running out of steam.

NEPTUNE ARIES

Neptune rules film, drugs, pharmaceuticals, spirituality and the arts. Aries is an independent star sign, the pioneer and trail-blazer who likes to be in it to win it. Will there be more individual experiences of spiritual bliss and transcendence? Or will there be more competition in Neptune-ruled areas of life? Certainly, it feels as if people might be searching for their own spiritual path.

Like Saturn in Aries, this combination isn't straightforward and doesn't feel especially comfortable. The little fishes of Neptune's realm are doing battle with Aries' mighty ram. Perhaps there will be literal fights and disputes over water.

SATURN/NEPTUNE ARIES

Saturn and Neptune are going to be working together in 2025 and this is significant. In June, July and August, they are extremely close in Aries, preparing the way for their epic conjunction in February 2026.

A Saturn–Neptune conjunction takes place approximately once every thirty-six years. The last time the conjunction took place, it fell in earth sign Capricorn in 1989. One of the most obvious symbols was the fall of the Berlin Wall, which had divided West and East Germany for years. Saturn is the planet of boundaries and Neptune dissolves what it touches.

Together, these two planets are often about socialist ideals and new political ideologies emerging. There can be a deep commitment to morality and a strong social conscience. The discipline of the spiritual path is emphasised and Saturn can help to turn Neptune's dreams into reality. There can be a turning away from materialism and a calling to a life of spirit.

Wherever Aries falls in your horoscope, there may be a theme of sacrifice or surrender. You might be on a deeply spiritual path or decide to devote your life to your beliefs or ideals. You may be committed to a cause that's dear to your heart.

At its best, use Saturn and Neptune together to preserve the arts or to pursue a creative, compassionate or charitable vocation. Be wary of falling into fear or doubt as there is a negative emphasis to this combination. Saturn and Neptune together can be a symbol of guilt or shame. Don't let addictions spiral out of control and instead, put your faith in healing and miracles. Practise self-forgiveness and remember that finding peace and contentment is an inner process.

II

RADICAL COMMUNICATION

Uranus is the innovator and awakener in astrology. In 2025, Uranus will be in air sign Gemini from 7 July to 8 November. Uranus will move back into Gemini next year in April 2026, where it will remain until 2032/2033. It's a new wave of air sign energy and experimental Uranus could feel at home in Gemini, the star sign of communication. This feels great for new technologies, communicating with outer space, new discoveries and inventions.

Uranus is a radical influence and this could bring back a wave of free speech, not being blocked for what you want to say. Perhaps, a new language will be discovered or there will be a flurry of twins being born.

There could be a revolution in transport as this is Gemini's realm. Electric cars are an obvious symbol for Uranus in Gemini, as Uranus is linked to electricity. And cars that drive themselves. Maybe we'll start jetting around the world in little mobile pods that ride the airwaves.

There are likely to be further developments in brain chips turning humans into computers and major advances in speech recognition technology. Wherever technology can push back the boundaries of what's possible, outrageous and radical Uranus will want to make it happen.

This combination feels speedy. On a personal level, you could expand your knowledge or learning at record speed. New records could be set around super-human feats of intelligence. We might be introduced to a new robot with amazing skills.

Use the internet to boost your potential but don't forget the human touch. Teacher or student, stay connected to life and your fellow human beings.

ECLIPSE CYCLES

Eclipses are not by their nature good or bad. They can sweep in and move things forwards, sometimes at a fast rate. Wherever the eclipses fall tend to be areas of your life where there's change and accelerated growth. In ancient times, before people learned to predict them, eclipses were feared as they would seem to happen out of the blue. You can imagine how scary it must have been when the sky went suddenly dark and the shadow of the Moon blocked out the light of the Sun.

Later, eclipses came to be seen as an omen that there was going to be a significant change in leadership. This is often true today. For example, in 2022 during the Taurus/Scorpio eclipse cycle. Queen Elizabeth II (Sun Taurus) died meaning that her son became King Charles III (Sun Scorpio).

On a personal level, eclipses coincide with an opportunity to sweep out the old in order to prepare the space for something fresh and new to emerge.

To understand eclipses more fully, the language and symbolism of the eclipse can act as a guide. There are other planetary eclipses but they're rarely used in horoscopes – the eclipses of the Sun and Moon are most important. These two main types of eclipse can be observed from Earth. In a lunar eclipse, Earth is between the Sun and the Moon. In a solar eclipse, the Moon is between the Sun and Earth. When the lights – the Sun and Moon – are eclipsed you are in the dark and events are hidden and shadowy. Secrets emerge and what's unknown comes to light a few days later. As an eclipse involves three bodies, the Sun, the Moon and the Earth, this may represent a 'triangle' situation in your life where one person loses out allowing another person to take advantage.

Eclipses are also a time when the pendulum of fate can swing dramatically – this may feel both exhilarating and scary. Sometimes, change happens close to the eclipse date, while at other times, the influence of an eclipse can last until the next eclipse approximately six months later. An eclipse has most impact when it falls within two degrees of a planet or angle in your birth chart. Very often, an event close to the eclipse date sets the wheels of change in motion and the eclipse energy plays out over the next few weeks or months.

Eclipses take place in cycles that usually last between eighteen to twenty-four months. What can happen is you get a run of eclipses triggering key points in your birth chart and your life shifts significantly within that period. When you look back on the past, you invariably see that major turning points in your life, moments of destiny, coincide with important eclipse cycles.

This year, there will be four eclipses taking place. It's worth taking note of the eclipse dates and preparing for them. Know that these are times at which you're likely to be on a roller-coaster experiencing the highs and lows of life. So, unsurprisingly, these are not ideal dates on which to plan major events. Instead, wait to see what happens when the shadow of the eclipse lifts. It's usually wise to wait a few days after an eclipse before making a major decision. I have added the degrees below to show where they are taking place, so you can check your own horoscopes in relation to them if you are interested.

VIRGO/PISCES ECLIPSES

- Lunar eclipse [25 Pisces 41] – 18 Sept 2024
- **Lunar eclipse [23 Virgo 57] – 14 March 2025**
- **Lunar eclipse [15 Pisces 23] – 7 Sept 2025**
- **Solar eclipse [29 Virgo 05] – 21 Sept 2025**
- Lunar eclipse [12 Virgo 54] – 3 March 2026
- Lunar eclipse [4 Pisces 54] – 28 August 2026
- Lunar eclipse [2 Virgo 06] – 20 February 2027

The major eclipse cycle in 2025 takes place in the star signs Pisces and Virgo. This cycle started in September 2024 and completes in February 2027.

Look out for Pisces and Virgo celebrities being in the news more than usual. Plus, it could be a pivotal couple of years for you if you're a Sun Virgo or Sun Pisces.

There are three eclipses here in 2025: two Full Moon lunar eclipses – one in Virgo on 14 March and one in Pisces on 7 September – plus, a New Moon solar eclipse in Virgo on 21 September.

PREVIOUS VIRGO/
PISCES ECLIPSE CYCLES

March 2006 to February 2008

September 1987 to August 1989

March 1969 to February 1971

The Virgo–Pisces axis highlights themes of service and sacrifice and taps you into the rituals of everyday life.

Virgo likes to keep busy and be useful and is the star sign linked to order. Pisces is a dreamer and prefers to flow through life. The Virgo–Pisces axis is a reminder to be grateful for what you have and to understand that less is sometimes more. Consider where there's a spiritual or devotional element in your life. This axis is linked to prayer as well as daily rituals.

Food and harvest are Virgo themes and Pisces rules the sea and liquids. The focus is on what we share with each other, how the Earth feeds and nourishes us, how we create a sustainable environment and how we care for the vulnerable in our society.

ARIES/LIBRA ECLIPSES

- Solar eclipse [29 Aries 50] – 20 April 2023
- Solar eclipse [21 Libra 08] – 14 October 2023
- Lunar eclipse [5 Libra 07] – 25 March 2024
- Solar eclipse [19 Aries 24] – 8 April 2024

- Solar eclipse [10 Libra 04] – 2 October 2024
- **Solar eclipse [9 Aries 00] – 29 March 2025**

The Aries/Libra eclipse cycle began in March 2023 and completes in March 2025.

Relationships are a major theme during this eclipse cycle. Aries is the first sign of the zodiac representing the ego and the self, while Libra is the star sign linked to relating. It's you versus them. The challenge may be how to keep your identity strong when you're in relationship with other people, both personally and professionally. Yet, the deeper learning about yourself comes from seeing and understanding yourself in relation to others. When you dive deep into love or any significant partnership in your life, you hold up a mirror revealing who you are.

What was noticeable during this eclipse cycle is that the majority of the eclipses were Solar or New Moon eclipses. Therefore, the theme of independence or finding yourself may ring true. There's one final eclipse in this cycle, a New Moon solar eclipse on 29 March. Following your own path, whether in a relationship or not, could be a major theme. Also, fighting for your rights or for the underdog.

Notice who comes into your life on or around the eclipse. Life isn't meant to be lived alone and it's the people you meet and the connections you build that often determine the course of your life.

PREVIOUS ARIES/
LIBRA ECLIPSE CYCLES

April 2004 to March 2006

April 1986 to October 1987

October 1967 to September 1969

This isn't just about relationships, however, because Aries and Libra are ruled by the planets Mars and Venus respectively. Therefore, this eclipse cycle could be said to be a symbol of war (Mars) and peace (Venus), love (Venus) and hate (Mars). And, tragically, it's been a time of new wars emerging around the globe.

Also, this represents the masculine (Mars) and feminine (Venus) principles. Issues around gender have been foreground during this eclipse cycle.

Astrology mirrors the duality in the world, as seen by the opposite star signs, which are reflected during eclipses. Yet, astrology teaches us to find a way to work with the opposing elements and learn from each side of the axis. There are times when we need to find a way to merge opposite principles, to see how they complement one another. Also, to be able to accept the differences between people and not to take advantage of others or call people out as 'wrong' because of this.

THE LUNAR NODES:

THE PATH OF DESTINY

The Lunar Nodes are the points where the Moon's path crosses the ecliptic – the Sun's path in the sky. Karmic points in astrology, the Nodes are also known as the Dragon's Head and Tail.

In your birth chart, the nodes reveal your soul purpose, your destiny in this lifetime. Whichever sign and house you find the North Node in, the South Node is always in the opposite sign and house.

North Node Pisces

South Node Virgo

12 January 2025 to 26 July 2026

The placing of the North Node is what you're striving towards or aiming for in this lifetime. It's your life lesson, your destiny and your major area of learning. The South Node is said to be where you retreat to, your comfort zone, your habitual place. In traditional astrology, it can indicate your downfall and what's not good for you. It's what you need to release and let go of. If you believe in past lives, it's thought that you're stuck in your South Node destiny until you are able to break free, stop repeating the same patterns and move on.

From 17 July 2023 to 12 January 2025, the Lunar Nodes were moving back across the Aries/Libra axis of the zodiac. Yet, as 2025 gets underway, there's a major shift as the North Node moves into Pisces and the South Node moves into Virgo. This is where the karmic Nodes will remain until 26 July 2026.

Nodal cycles last for approximately eighteen or nineteen years. It can be helpful to look back to previous nodal cycles to make sense of where these powerful indicators fall in your horoscope. You can see patterns playing out that repeat through time, the beginning and end of major chapters in your life.

These are the last dates when the North Node was in Pisces and the South Node in Virgo: June 2006 to December 2007, December 1987 to May 1989, April 1969 to November 1970, July 1950 to March 1952, and so on.

The Lunar Nodes are an integral part of the eclipse cycle. In fact, it's said not to be a true eclipse if the nodes aren't close to the eclipse degree.

N.B. For the astrology nerds, there are two types of node – True Node, which is more accurate as it wobbles back and forward, and also the Mean Node, which is simplified and always in retrograde motion. They don't differ by much but I prefer to use the True Node.

SLOW DOWN

Mercury retrograde is an astrological phenomenon that has become mainstream news. People who know little about astrology have often heard of this common event, which the media like to run stories about.

MERCURY RETROGRADE

15 March [09 Aries 33]
to 7 April [26 Pisces 50]

18 July [15 Leo 33] to 11 August [04 Leo 17]

9 November [06 Sagittarius 52]
to 29 November [20 Scorpio 43]

Mercury is the trickster planet, the messenger and rules all forms of communication. Approximately three times a year for three weeks at a time, Mercury retreats through the zodiac.

This can coincide with communication chaos, technical glitches, misunderstandings and delays. So it is not advisable to buy technology or transport when Mercury's retrograde as things are more likely to go wrong.

Mercury is one of the planets linked to money and gives its name to the markets and merchandise. Mercury retrograde phases often coincide with topsy-turvy times in the money markets.

Extreme weather is another common feature of the Mercury retrograde phases, bringing transport chaos. And there are numerous examples of projects and major world events which haven't gone smoothly during Mercury retrograde.

Often, you have to start over or begin again once Mercury ceases being retrograde and resumes moving forward through the zodiac. Therefore, when Mercury's retrograde, hold your horses and delay the big decisions if possible. If you do have to sign a contract, read the small print carefully.

There are many ways you can use the Mercury retrograde phase to good effect though, as looking backwards is not always a bad thing. It's wise to focus on the 're'-words, e.g:

- review your current situation
- retrace your steps
- rework your ideas, revise your plans
- reflect and reconsider your options
- rethink your next steps
- re-connect with people from your past
- read and re-read the small print, pay attention to the details
- rest, relax and retreat

Mercury retrograde is a time when you can slow down and look at life from a different angle, a fresh perspective. It can be a powerful time of inner growth and learning, rather than out-and-out action. It's a positive period to slow down or go on retreat. You may learn from your mistakes too.

Each Mercury retrograde phase is different depending which star sign it takes place in. This year Mercury retreats predominantly through the fire signs, Aries, Leo and Sagittarius. Fire signs are renowned for impulsive behaviour, so be cautious what you leap into leading up to the Mercury Retrogrades and be wary of burn-out too. Mercury moves back into emotional water signs in March/April and November, encouraging you to get back in flow.

When Mercury turns and once more moves forward through the zodiac, this can indicate a light-bulb moment when ideas that have been gestating throughout the retrograde phase spring to life. It's a positive time to listen out for new information and chase things up.

VENUS'S ATTRACTION

Venus is the female principle and one of the two best planets in astrology. Wherever Venus goes, happiness and popularity come along for the ride. Venus dances through the zodiac, bringing beauty, adoration and gifts your way. Here's when you have your turn with Venus gracing your star sign in 2025:

- Venus Aquarius – until 3 January
- Venus Pisces – 3 January to 4 February
- Venus Aries – 4 February to 27 March
- Venus Pisces – 27 March to 30 April
- Venus Aries – 30 April to 6 June
- Venus Taurus – 6 June to 4 July
- Venus Gemini – 4 July to 31 July
- Venus Cancer – 31 July to 25 August
- Venus Leo – 25 August to 19 September 19
- Venus Virgo – 19 September to 13 October
- Venus Libra – 13 October to 6 November

- Venus Scorpio – 6 November to 30 November
- Venus Sagittarius – 30 November to 24 December
- Venus Capricorn – from 24 December

VENUS RETROGRADE

In order to change from evening to morning star, Venus becomes invisible as she journeys back through the zodiac. This is a powerful phase when Venus disappears from sight and re-emerges reborn – its retrograde phase in astrology.

Venus is the planet linked to women and has come to represent the feminine ideal that's sweet, kind and charming – but there are many aspects to Venus. Venus is the archetype of woman, which not only includes sweetheart, but also sexual lover and warrior. The Mayans saw Venus as a warrior goddess when the planet emerged as morning star.

VENUS RETROGRADE

2 March to 13 April

In astrology, Venus rules love and relating, money, beauty, art and pleasure. When a planet turns retrograde, its energy is said to be weakened. Therefore, it's not the best time to pursue Venus-related matters. Venus retrograde is not the time to marry, have expensive beauty treatments, cosmetic surgery or make major purchases or investments.

Sometimes, you're parted from the one you love when Venus is in its retrograde phase. Or love goes quiet. Some astrologers suggest that if you fall in love during Venus retrograde, it won't last.

Yet, it's not so black and white. It might mean that a relationship takes longer to get off the ground. Or that you both have doubts at first or the timing's not right. If you're in a rocky relationship, this could be when you realise that your relationship is going backwards and you want to call the whole thing off. Yet, astrological advice would be to wait until Venus turns direct before you make up your mind. Venus retrograde can symbolise a change of heart. As with all retrograde phases, Venus retrograde connects you to the past so you may hear from an ex or a childhood sweetheart. If you still have fond feelings for someone in your past, this is a good time to get back in touch, although put off the big decisions until Venus turns direct.

Venus retrograde can be an ideal time to reassess what you value in life, where your desires lie and recognise who or what's important to you. When Venus is in retreat, this is an ideal time to contemplate love, consider what it means to you, and whether you're in the right relationship. It's the time for inner work and reflection rather than actively pursuing a love relationship.

Venus turns retrograde approximately every eighteen months. This year, Venus will be retrograde from 2 March to 13 April. Here are the key dates:

- Venus enters Aries – 4 February
- Venus turns retrograde [10 Aries 50] – 2 March

- Venus returns to Pisces – 27 March
- Venus turns direct [24 Pisces 39] – 13 April
- Venus re-enters Aries – 30 April

This is an interesting retrograde phase because Venus turns retrograde in Aries, an independent star sign. It then moves back into romantic Pisces where Venus turns direct. You may sense the push-pull between wanting to be on your own and wanting to merge with another. Allow things to settle rather than rushing into a major decision.

MARS'S POWER

Mars is the action planet. When Mars is powerful, this symbolises desire, passion, a fighting spirit, physical activity, courage and daring. Mars wants to get from A to B as swiftly as possible. Direct action is Mars's domain, fierce and forceful. Mars rules the libido, the creative impulse. Therefore, it's helpful to know where Mars is in the zodiac. When Mars is in your star sign, it lends you motivation and ambition to get ahead. Here are Mars's movements in 2025:

- Mars Leo – until 6 January
- Mars Cancer – 6 January to 18 April
- Mars Leo – 18 April to 17 June
- Mars Virgo – 17 June to 6 August
- Mars Libra – 6 August to 22 September
- Mars Scorpio – 22 September to 4 November
- Mars Sagittarius – 4 November to 15 December
- Mars Capricorn – from 15 December

MARS RETROGRADE

Mars turns retrograde approximately once every two years. As 2025 opens, Mars is in its retrograde phase, which began on 6 December 2024 and lasts until 24 February. This could prove frustrating, especially if you're Aries or Scorpio, the star signs ruled by Mars. Also, Leo and Cancer, as it's here where Mars is retrograde.

MARS RETROGRADE

6 December 2024 to 24 February 2025

Mars retrograde is a time when you can't get ahead as fast as you would like. You may have to learn patience the hard way and it's wise to take care of your physical health. Be wary of being overly arrogant or confident when Mars is in retreat. Beware the wrath of hubris. When Mars is retrograde, actively slow down so you avoid burn-out. Take your foot off the accelerator of life. Sometimes, when Mars is travelling backwards through the zodiac, you realise that you don't have control or you're not the one with the power. Decision-making may not be straightforward when Mars is in retreat. Learn to follow in this period rather than lead.

When Mars is retrograde, you might feel demotivated or lacking in energy. Or perhaps you end up running fast, charging into something new and going in the wrong direction. Don't waste your energy unnecessarily during the retrograde phase and think carefully about what you say yes to. Look after your body, keep fit but don't overdo it. Avoid angry individuals. Experiment with pulling back and adopt the mantra 'less is more'.

Mars is confident in Leo but be wary of hubris when Mars is retrograde here as the year begins. Mars retreats back into Cancer, a star sign it's not comfortable in. Yet it may be wise to nest and tend to your wounds before you get ready to be back out in the world.

Perhaps your family need you in the first two months of the year or you want to hibernate and stay home more than usual. Be wary of being overly moody and try not to turn your anger in on yourself.

There are always vital lessons to learn when an inner planet is retrograde. Therefore, notice what happens if you're halted in your efforts or you're on the wrong track. Rework your strategy, retreat your army and get ready for action once Mars turns direct.

Mars is retrograde from 6 December 2024 to 24 February 2025. Here are the key dates:

- Mars enters Leo – 4 November 2024
- Mars turns retrograde [06 Leo 10] – 6 December 2024

- Mars returns to Cancer – 6 January 2025
- Mars turns direct [17 Cancer 01] – 24 February 2025
- Mars re-enters Leo – 18 April 2025

THE LUNAR CYCLE:

IN TUNE WITH THE MOON

One of the easiest ways to be in flow with astrology is to be in step with the lunar cycle. In ancient times, there were thirteen months in the lunar calendar. The word 'month' derives from the old English word for 'Moon'. Each Moon cycle lasts for approximately twenty-eight-and-a-half days. When you first catch sight of the crescent Moon, make a wish because new Moon wishes can come true.

The beginning of a New Moon cycle is a perfect time to start something new. When the sliver of a 'fingernail Moon' is in the sky, sow seeds, launch a project, take the initiative. At this time, the Sun and Moon sit next to one another in the same sign of the zodiac. The following two weeks favour dynamic energy when you see things grow – the waxing phase of the moon. Then, you reach the Full Moon phase, a time of completion, the culmination of the lunar cycle. This is the perfect time to celebrate and acknowledge what you've achieved. At this point, the Sun and Moon oppose each other in opposite signs of the zodiac.

The subsequent two weeks is when the moon begins to wane. It's a time to consolidate what you started, complete deadlines and begin to release and let go of what's no longer needed or helpful in your life. The period directly before the next lunar cycle heralds the dark of the moon when the moon isn't visible at all in the night sky. Traditionally, this is the time to rest and retreat in readiness for the next New Moon and a wave of fresh energy.

Here are your New Moon and Full Moon dates for 2025. Note that the eclipses are included, and these are a different type of Moon event. The solar eclipse is a New Moon and the lunar eclipse is a Full Moon. Refer to the eclipse page above for guidance, also your horoscope.

- Full Moon – 13 January [24 Cancer 00]
- New Moon – 29 January [09 Aquarius 51]
- Full Moon – 12 February [24 Leo 06]
- New Moon – 28 February [09 Pisces 41]
- Total lunar eclipse – 14 March [23 Virgo 57]
- Partial solar eclipse – 29 March [09 Aries 00]
- Full Moon – 13 April [23 Libra 20]
- New Moon – 27 April [07 Taurus 47]
- Full Moon – 12 May [22 Scorpio 13]
- New Moon – 27 May [06 Gemini 06]
- Full Moon – 11 June [20 Sagittarius 39]
- New Moon – 25 June [04 Cancer 08]
- Full Moon – 10 July [18 Capricorn 50]

- New Moon – 24 July [02 Leo 08]
- Full Moon – 9 August [17 Aquarius 00]
- New Moon – 23 August [00 Virgo 23]
- Total lunar eclipse – 7 September [15 Pisces 23]
- Partial solar eclipse – 21 September [29 Virgo 05]
- Full Moon – 7 October [14 Aries 08] *Super Moon
- New Moon – 21 October [28 Libra 22]
- Full Moon – 5 November [13 Taurus 23] *Super Moon
- New Moon – 20 November [28 Scorpio 12]
- Full Moon – 4 December [13 Gemini 04] *Super Moon
- New Moon – 20 December [28 Sagittarius 25]

*Super Moons are when the Moon is closest to Earth and more beautiful to behold.

ARIES

YOUR 2025 HOROSCOPE

ARIES RULERSHIPS

ZODIAC SYMBOL: THE RAM

RULING PLANET: MARS — GOD OF WAR,
PLANET OF ACTION

MODE/ELEMENT: CARDINAL FIRE —
INITIATING, FIRECRACKER, GO-GETTING,
FEISTY

COLOUR: RED

ARCHETYPE: THE HERO, THE PIONEER

YOUR TOP TIPS FOR 2025

USE YOUR VOICE, START A
CAREER IN COMMUNICATION

INVEST IN PROPERTY OR YOUR FAMILY

EMBARK ON A JOURNEY
OF SELF-DISCOVERY

FIND YOUR FAITH; GO ON A HEALTH
OR SPIRITUAL RETREAT

DEVELOP A NEW IDEOLOGY;
UNLEASH YOUR INNER ACTIVIST

♈

COMMUNICATION AND COMMUNITY

The biggest planet in the universe and the best planet in astrology, Jupiter, is in air sign Gemini as the year begins and will remain here until 9 June. Wherever Jupiter goes, opportunity and good fortune follow. Therefore, you're wise to make the most of the area of your horoscope where Jupiter resides.

Jupiter in Gemini is the linguist and wordsmith and breathes fresh air into your life. Gemini rules communication in your horoscope, as well as tuition and learning. Jupiter's position is ideal for all forms of communication – talking and writing, sharing ideas and information, making new friends and learning new skills. Perhaps this is the year you go back to school?

This awakens the social side of your nature too, as Gemini not only rules communication but your local community. It's linked to your siblings, your close relatives and your neighbours. You may be raring to go, ready to be more social and get to know people better who live close by. Plus, there are some lovely connections to lucky Jupiter from the Sun and inner planets as they move through social Aquarius and your star sign Aries. Great dates for social occasions and get-togethers are 30 January and 3 February. Join in with a group or find your tribe.

The only proviso here is that your ruling planet Mars is

retrograde until 24 February. This indicates that not everything will work out at the start of the year and you're wise to take your foot off the accelerator of life. Stick to what you know rather than start something new. Perhaps you're caught up in a stop-start scenario. You're not in control or in charge when your planet Mars is in retreat. Mars rules energy and drive, so Mars retrograde is a time to slow things down rather than speed things up. Less is more is a wise mantra and there's no rush in the first few months of 2025.

In March and April, two other planets, communication planet Mercury and the planet of relating Venus, are on go slow. What retrograde planets are good for is going over old ground, reviewing your options, research or study. Use the first few months of 2025 well by focusing on your inner life and intellectual development.

Fast forward to 6 April, 5 May and 5 June and you have luck on your side as Jupiter aligns with the light of the Sun, talk planet Mercury and Venus, all in your star sign Aries. Use your opportunities on or around these key dates and you could attract the right kind of attention. This is when you're at your most popular and it's a good time to make new friends and influence people. Use the New Moon in Gemini on 27 May to launch a neighbourhood initiative.

Another stand-out date is 8 June, when Mercury and Jupiter align in Gemini, making it an ideal date to take an exam or pass a test. You could apply for university or sign up to an evening class. This combination is great for any form of trade, even setting up a car boot sale or market stall.

This may be the year you become a voice-over artist or crossword writer. Perhaps, you launch a podcast, learn journalism or become a spokesperson for a charity or a neighbourhood group. Whatever your bag, use your voice to the best of your ability.

The air signs are more prominent from this year onwards, as this is where the modern planets are moving to. Power planet Pluto, linked to transformation and psychoanalysis, is in air sign Aquarius, where it will remain for the next twenty years. Aquarius represents the unions, group consensus, community and associations and coming together to serve the people. At its best, Pluto in Aquarius is people power and you may be one of those at the forefront of change moving forward. If you're a typical Aries, you're a fighter and radical, a disruptor of the status quo. Perhaps, you've left a corporate job or you're on the verge of doing so. You might be keen to move into a new role, one that's ethical, linked to sustainability or humanitarian or environmental goals.

There's another major shift this year because from 7 July to 8 November, the planet of innovation and change Uranus enters Gemini. This is where it will take up residence from April 2026 for the next seven years. Uranus is linked to broadcasting and modern technologies. Therefore, what you get involved with while Jupiter is in Gemini could lead you into new technologies or working in a new or futuristic environment. You could be propelled at top speed into a new and exciting initiative.

August is potentially the most significant month for new developments, when Uranus in Gemini teams up with key planets in your star sign Aries on 12 August and 29 August. Where are you going to be at the forefront of new inventions or modern trends?

HOME AND FAMILY

At the start of 2025 your ruling planet Mars is retrograde in Cancer. This means it is a time when it's harder to make progress at home or with regard to family. But never fear, as the second half of the year is when things are likely to take off for you in these areas.

Mars first entered Cancer on 4 September 2024, remaining there until 4 November. Then, Mars turned retrograde on 6 December and returns to Cancer on 6 January this year. Perhaps it's been a disruptive period for family affairs, your home's undergoing renovations or a property transaction has been delayed. Don't worry, because a turning point comes on 24 February when Mars turns direct. Use this date to be assertive and push things through. Chase up a member of your family or start over in some way, linked to your home life or domestic situation.

Mars remains in Cancer until 18 April, confirming that this is a significant area of your life in 2025. It's likely that you'll have some key resolutions or intentions at the start of the year to improve your home or family life. You may just have to be patient and wait until the middle of the year to see your plans start to come to fruition.

Jupiter changes star sign on 9 June and moves into Cancer. Jupiter will remain here for one year until 30 June 2026. This is an important transit of Jupiter for you, as it turns the cosmic spotlight towards your home and family, your past and roots. When Jupiter's in this sector of your horoscope, it's a classic time to move home and expand your family or the place where you live.

With Jupiter's foreign theme, you might be planning a move

abroad. Or perhaps a get-together with family who live scattered around the world or in a different part of the country. A big family celebration is a good way to make the most of Jupiter's move into Cancer.

During the middle of the year, there's a lot going on in this part of your horoscope. The stand-out dates are 24 June, when there's a lucky Sun–Jupiter conjunction in Cancer, and 12 August, when there's a loving Venus–Jupiter conjunction in Cancer. Both are great dates for celebrating an anniversary or family wedding. Alternatively, for investing in property or selling your home.

June, July and August would be the perfect time to catch up with people from your past, to remember your roots and where you come from. You might choose to add to your family, whether this involves children or pets, the addition of a step-family or living within a community. Jupiter works in synchronous ways, so it's important that you put yourself in its path. Say yes to a new home or family-related opportunity that opens up when Jupiter begins its journey through Cancer.

You may find a way to work from home or start a business or charity, if that's on your wish list. The key dates are 22 June, 12 September and 8 October. Or, perhaps you're helping a member of your family find work or get on the property ladder.

Later in the year is when your finances could prosper, and this may be linked to a home move or family initiative. The lucky dates are 24 October, 28 October, 17 November, 26 November and 6 December.

There is one other period in the year which feels important with regard to home and family, and this is 15 June to 19 June. Between these two dates, Jupiter in Cancer squares up to Saturn and Neptune in your star sign Aries. You may be trying extra hard to make something work out during this time. Yet be wary of your motivations and check in with yourself whether guilt or fear are the driving force for change. Perhaps this will show you where you can't break free from past ties. Or you realise there's some work to do if you're to improve your relationship with family or have the home situation that's right for you.

A NEW IDENTITY

Another major planetary shift in 2025 involves the planet Saturn returning to your star sign Aries for the first time in thirty years, from 25 May to 1 September. It will return to Aries next year, on 14 February 2026, and remain in your star sign until April 2028.

Saturn is the planet of responsibility and authority, linked to dedication and long-term plans. Therefore, consider where you're ready to make a major commitment. This is about your personal goals and aims, your image and profile. Saturn in Aries could help you flex your levels of self-discipline. Perhaps you'll commit to a new daily habit. Or you start a course of personal study that will complete in two to three years' time. Draw up a plan once Saturn is in Aries and look to the future.

Saturn in Aries teams up with Uranus in Gemini on 12 August. This combination favours using your experience and knowledge in a new or innovative way. How can you implement what you've learned in the past and share what you know with more people? Perhaps this relates to an online class or writing an ebook.

What you need to be wary of with Saturn in your star sign is that you don't become a harsh taskmaster. Notice if you're trying to take on too much or you're working overly hard. Be aware that this is possible and keep close tabs on your attitude, your health and well-being.

Saturn is the planet linked to work and ambition and needs a mountain to climb, something to work towards. There's a theme of the 'lone wolf' when Saturn's in Aries and being your own boss often suits your Aries nature. You're likely to be most successful when your goals and aims are personal and mean something to you, rather than working hard for someone else. Yet, note that Saturn's nature is very different from your own fast and furious approach to life. Slow and steady wins the race when Saturn's in the driving seat. For example, Saturn in Aries can be helpful if you're training for a marathon or planning to climb a mountain. It's the work you put in day in, day out that will stand you in good stead for the future.

Also, there may be times this year when you need to be patient if things don't work out the way you want them to. For example, the Sun's move into your star sign on 20 March heralds the equinox, the start of spring in the northern hemisphere. This is often a period when you're keen to set new goals, get fit or engage fully with life. However, this year, as talk planet Mercury turns retrograde in Aries on 15 March and remains on go slow until 7 April, this isn't the best time to make a major decision or start something new. Instead, you're wise to wait until Mercury returns to Aries on 16 April to get things moving.

Mercury remains in Aries until 10 May and is joined by the planet of relating, Venus, from 30 April to 6 June. What's significant here is that both planets are social, which indicates that getting ahead may require teamwork or partnership. Trying to go it alone isn't likely to bring you success. Though this could go against your natural inclination as Aries is the first sign of the zodiac. If you're typical of your star sign, you're used to walking your own path in life and doing things your way.

Plus, there's been a run of powerful solar eclipses, portals of change, in Aries during your birthday month for the last three years – in 2023, 2024 and, on 29 March this year, you have a turbo-powered solar eclipse calling you forward. A solar eclipse is a like a New Moon with rocket fuel behind it – a symbol of new beginnings amped up to the max. Sometimes, during powerful eclipses in your star sign, you grab your five minutes of fame or get yourself noticed, seen or heard. It's a time when you want to be more Aries – i.e. assertive, courageous and self-centred. There's a strong focus on your ability to make progress and develop yourself as an individual. However, don't wait for an eclipse wake-up call to change something that actually needs addressing, such as a health issue or difficult relationship, as the power of eclipses is not always predictable and they can coincide with drama or crisis.

There's another interesting development, which involves Neptune also moving into Aries. You will experience the effects of this from 30 March to 22 October. Neptune moves out of Aries later this year but will return on 26 January 2026. Then, Neptune remains in the most personal sector of your horoscope for another twelve years. This can be deeply creative or spiritual as Neptune taps you into your inner source.

This is a year with the potential to bring you a new landscape and, perhaps, a new sense of identity or purpose. How you see yourself and how others perceive you may alter in 2025. When Saturn and Neptune are working together in June, July and August, at its best, you'll become more idealistic. What you thought were important values in your life could change. For example, you may be less interested in material status or achievement. This could be the year when you reconnect with your inner activist and your desire to make a difference as an individual. Alternatively, if you've fallen prey to conspiracy theories or you've lost your way, Saturn's move into Aries could be a helpful reality check.

What's important for you in 2025 is to have something to believe in or something to engage with that gives your life meaning and purpose.

SPIRITUAL PATH, HEALTH AND WELL-BEING

The process of inner development may be something you're already aware of as you move into 2025. This is because Saturn and Neptune have been in Pisces and the most private sector of your horoscope in recent years. Neptune's been here since 2012 and Saturn since March 2023. Pisces' co-ruler is Neptune, god of the sea, linked to the collective unconscious, a spiritual and compassionate influence. When key planets are in Pisces, this turns your attention inward, as Pisces rules your inner life. It's about retreat and reflection, quiet time and solitude.

In 2025, Saturn remains in Pisces up until 25 May and returns to Pisces on 1 September. Neptune is here up until 30 March and returns to Pisces on 22 October. During these periods, it's a good idea to make the most of these influences. For example, this could be a significant year in your life linked to religion, meditation or spirituality. It could call out your inner shaman. The effect of this is likely to be profound for you early in the year, as the North Node (see page 37) enters Pisces on 12 January, remaining there until 26 July 2026. The Nodes are linked to a call of destiny that continue to speak until you feel called to take action.

In addition, the inner planets Mercury and Venus spend half of their retrograde phases in Pisces in 2025. As previously mentioned, Mercury is retrograde from 15 March to 7 April, and Venus is retrograde from 2 March to 13 April. This means that both planets spend longer than usual in Pisces and interact numerous times with the North Node, Saturn and Neptune. This is an unusual amount of planetary activity in one sector of your horoscope for the first four months of 2025, from January through to April. The power of this profound Pisces' influence could lead to a revelation or awakening early in the year. This might be in a spiritual context. Or, perhaps something which helps you learn more about yourself and the wider universe. 'Find yourself' could be the mantra to adopt, if you're willing to immerse yourself fully in this Pisces wave of energy.

When planets are in Pisces, it's about caring for others as well as caring for yourself. You may decide to step into a role that takes you into a prison, hospital, hospice or refugee centre. Though there may be a specific reason why you need to slow down in this first third of the year, perhaps due to illness, low energy or your role as a carer.

Planets in Pisces are also a reminder that change starts on the inside. This means actively working on your mindset and developing your trust and faith in life. The universe is always talking to you. And, when you listen to your intuition or hunches, things start to shift. There's an inner knowingness that you can develop and will help guide you. It's about doing what feels right rather than trying to work things out in your head and relying on the power of logic alone. Taking action and diving into new experiences may be what's needed here, which is, after all, your Aries' default mode.

The theme of second chances is strong and you may feel closely connected to the cycle of karma and what's gone before. This can relate to your past in this lifetime or even past lives.

What's important to note is that Pisces is the last sign of the zodiac, whereas your star sign Aries is the first sign of the zodiac. Pisces is a boundless place that has little to do with the ego or individual effort. It's the places in life where you lose yourself, where you feel connected to the universe and what lies beyond the everyday. But be wary of losing yourself in the wrong way – for example, drink, drugs or addiction. Instead, learn to surrender to life and find faith in prayer. Or use music, poetry or art as your creative or inner muse.

There's a sense that what you give, you receive in return when planets are in Pisces. This is the deeper message of the Virgo–Pisces axis of the zodiac, where the eclipses fall this year.

There are two powerful Full Moon lunar eclipses this year – in Virgo on 14 March and in Pisces on 7 September. Plus, your ruling planet Mars is in Virgo from 17 June to 6 August. The Virgo–Pisces axis is about your work and health, your lifestyle and routine. Also, being of service to others, whether this is via your religion or a volunteering role. It's these key areas of your life where you're being asked to be curious and notice where life's calling you.

This year, there are two New Moons in Virgo, which is unusual. The first New Moon in Virgo falls on 23 August. This would be a positive date in the year to set new health or lifestyle resolutions. The second New Moon is a solar eclipse in Virgo on 21 September, the day before the Equinox. This eclipse cycle began in September 2024 and continues until February 2027. Sometimes, eclipse events arrive with a bang. Other times, you notice signposts or synchronicities leading you down a new path.

Whether 2025 is the year you change religion, start a spiritual practice, go on retreat, do a detox or prioritise your health and well-being, the planets are encouraging you to care for yourself deeply and nurture and nourish your inner source.

MONEY AND TAKING RISKS

The planet of change and the unexpected Uranus has been in Taurus, and the money sector of your horoscope, since 2018. Uranus rules all things modern. In Taurus, this is the digital revolution, the rise of crypto-currencies and technological advancements. You may have been riding the wave of new technologies over the last few years. Whatever your personal situation, things cannot remain the same when Uranus is active. Uranus isn't about financial stability. Instead, it often coincides with the highs and lows of life, triggering big wins but potentially losses too.

Last year, 2024, power planet Pluto left Capricorn – another earth sign, along with Taurus and Virgo – and your career and vocation sector, where it's been since 2008. Whether you became a plutocrat and boosted your wealth or you crashed into debt and went bankrupt, it could have been a time of highs and lows for your career path.

This year, Uranus is leaving Taurus and will be out of your money sector from 7 July to 8 November. It returns at the end of the year but come 26 April 2026, you'll be saying goodbye to Uranus in your money sector for the next eighty years. If you're looking for financial stability or you're tired of living on the edge financially, Uranus changing star sign could be a good thing.

In astrology, money is linked to value and self-worth. The more you value yourself and your services, the easier it is to charge what you're worth and ensure you're paid fairly. This year, the Sun's move through Taurus from 19 April to 20 May could be helpful to shine a light on finances. Also, Venus's move through Taurus from 6 June to 4 July is a positive period for financial deals and transactions.

Fast forward to the end of the year and the theme of highs and lows returns. Firstly, be wary of financial dealings from 9–29 November when Mercury is retrograde. Mercury is linked to trade and the Mercury retrograde phases are often a time when the trading markets and stocks and shares go topsy-turvy.

Mercury will turn direct in Scorpio and your joint finance sector on 29 November – and when communication planet Mercury turns direct, this often brings new information to light. Plus, there's a lot of activity in your finance sector towards the end of the year. Key dates on which to make the right moves are 24 October, 28 October and 6 December, when you have lucky Jupiter on your side. Also, financial ventures could go well on 17 November and 26 November.

Unpredictable Uranus is unusually active during this period in the year, opposing the inner planets in Scorpio. These are the dates to avoid taking a financial risk: 19 November, 21 November, 30 November and 10 December. Uranus clashes are rash and impulsive and not great for leaping in. However, you are a Sun Aries, known for risk-taking, and the astrology towards the end of this year has a theme of 'double or quits'.

The judgement calls will be yours to make, but it's worth using the Jupiter dates well and avoiding the Uranus dates for investing. Perhaps, you'll be ready to ride the Uranus in Taurus's financial roller-coaster one more time before Uranus moves on.

You may have worked out how to make the most of Uranus's innovative and futuristic genius over the last few years. Alternatively, you may have had your fingers burnt one too many times. Your call, whether you go big or stay safe, as Uranus prepares to depart your personal money sector.

LOVE AND PASSION

In 2025, the focus is powerfully on you and your self-development, whether you're in a relationship or not. Yet, this doesn't mean nothing's happening when it comes to love. In fact, there's been a lot going on in your relationship sector recently, as the Aries/Libra eclipse cycle – which began in April 2023 and completes this year in March 2025 – is likely to have impacted not only your personal life but your relationships too. Eclipses accelerate growth as the wheel of fortune kicks in. When the eclipses highlight your relationship sector, relationships can start or end, sometimes dramatically.

Plus, Venus is linked to relationships in your horoscope, the goddess of love. And this year, Venus will be in your star sign for an unusually long time, from 4 February to 27 March, and again from 30 April to 6 June. Venus rules love and money, art and beauty – all the good things in life. When you have Venus in your star sign, you can attract attention and gain popularity. As Venus is in Aries not once but twice, this tells you that it's going to turn retrograde. Venus will be in retreat from 2 March to 13 April, and, for the first half of this retrograde phase, Venus is in your star sign Aries. The pivotal turning point comes on 23 March when the Sun and Venus unite in Aries, a passionate union. The Sun brings light, so themes of illumination and enlightenment are foreground. This date could prove to be a significant moment for a love relationship or for your own self-understanding and insight around love and what it means to you.

Traditionally, the Venus retrograde phase is not the time to engage with Venusian pursuits, i.e. don't marry, have cosmetic surgery or make a major investment. This is because you may regret your decision or choice once Venus is back up to speed. Sometimes, when Venus is retrograde, you go back to an ex or a childhood sweetheart comes into your life. Alternatively, there are major shifts within a relationship or you choose to spend time apart.

After the conjunction with the Sun, Venus starts to gain strength in its warrior phase. Venus brings wisdom and experience, when it emerges from the dark and into the light. Once Venus turns direct on 13 April, you may get a better idea about what someone else wants, and what you want too, when it comes to love. Plus, this coincides with your ruler Mars moving through Leo and your romance sector from 18 April to 17 June, an ideal time to chase after love and follow your passions.

The period when you're wise to slow things down again is 18 July to 11 August, as this is when communication planet Mercury is retrograde in Leo. Take the pace slow and don't hurry love.

Leo rules children in your horoscope as well as romance. It's all the things in life you 'give birth to'. Therefore, if you're a parent, stay focused on your children during the Mercury retrograde phase, without putting added pressure upon them. Use the turning point on 11 August to address any issues and discuss what comes to light.

Relationships peak again when Mars is in Libra and your relationship sector from 6 August to 22 September. This coincides with Venus in Leo from 25 August to 19 September. Finally, the love planet Venus moves into your relationship sector from 13 October to 6 November. The Full Moon in Aries on 7 October and the New Moon in Libra on 21 October could both be pivotal dates for love.

You may not have major planets shining a light on your love life in 2025, yet follow wherever the lovers of the heavens Venus and Mars go, and you may be pleasantly surprised by what arises.

RULING PLANET

It's important to know where your ruling planet Mars is moving through the zodiac. Mars rules action and get-up-and-go. It's a passionate and feisty force that shows you where to channel your energy and where best to crack on.

As the year begins, Mars is back on its long journey through water sign Cancer. As we have seen, at the start of the year on 6 January, Mars returns to Cancer where it spent two months towards the end of 2024, but in retrograde motion this time, until 18 April. As outlined in the 'Home and Family' section, your past and where you come from, also your connection to your home and family are influenced by Cancer, meaning that this period may be a sentimental and emotional time.

But on 18 April, Mars returns to fire sign Leo, where it turned retrograde on 6 December 2024, which is a creative placing for Mars. Mars in Leo tends to be confident and courageous. Find your passion, put play before work. Mars is in Leo until 17 June.

On 17 June, Mars moves into Virgo and your work and health sector until 6 August. This is when you may be more willing to get your head down and work hard. If there's a financial incentive for doing so, so much the better.

On 6 August, Mars enters Libra, your opposite star sign, until 22 September. This is a key period in the year to focus on love and relationships. In some relationships, personal or professional, you may not have as much power or control as you would like. Experiment with following rather than leading.

From 22 September until 4 November, Mars is in Scorpio, its other sign of rulership. Mars likes to be here, where it's laser-focused, obsessive and strong. You may dive deep into esotericism, tackle a taboo issue or work on improving your financial portfolio – check back to the key dates in the 'Money and Taking Risks' section.

From 4 November until 15 December, Mars is in fire sign Sagittarius, your travel and study sector. If you're keen to spread your wings and expand your horizons, you're in tune with your stars.

Finally, on 15 December, Mars enters earth sign Capricorn, the star sign at the peak of your horoscope, representing your career and vocation, your status and reputation. Power beckons during this transit and you're wise to rev up your ambitious nature once again.

LUCKY DATES

Mars turns direct – 24 February

Your New Moon Aries, eclipse power – 29 March

Sun Aries sextile Jupiter Gemini – 6 April

Mars enters Leo – 18 April

Venus Aries sextile Jupiter Gemini – 5 June

Mars Virgo sextile Jupiter Cancer – 22 June

Your Full Moon Aries, achievement/culmination – 7 October

Mars Scorpio trine Jupiter Cancer – 28 October

TAURUS

YOUR 2025 HOROSCOPE

TAURUS RULERSHIPS

ZODIAC SYMBOL: THE BULL

RULING PLANET: VENUS, GODDESS OF
LOVE, PLANET OF SENSUALITY

MODE/ELEMENT: FIXED EARTH –
DEPENDABLE, SECURITY-CONSCIOUS,
NATURE LOVING

COLOUR: GREEN, ALL COLOURS
OF THE EARTH

ARCHETYPE: EARTH MOTHER,
GOD/GODDESS OF ABUNDANCE

YOUR TOP TIPS FOR 2025

REVOLUTIONISE YOUR FINANCES,
BECOME A TECH GENIUS

FIND YOUR TRIBE, DEEPEN
YOUR COMMUNITY CONNECTIONS

LEARN SHAMANISM, EMBRACE
YOUR HEALING POWERS

PLAY AN ACTIVE ROLE IN POLITICS
OR SOCIAL CHANGE

PRACTISE MINDFULNESS,
EMBRACE SLOW LIVING

WORK AND MONEY

As the year begins, Jupiter is in air sign Gemini. Jupiter entered Gemini on 25 May 2024, where it remains until 9 June 2025. Wherever Jupiter goes, opportunity and good fortune follow. Therefore, you're wise to make the most of the area of your horoscope where Jupiter resides, and Gemini is the sign which rules money in your horoscope, including finances, assets, possessions and all that you value highly in life. During the first half of 2025, you could come across an opportunity to boost your finances or improve your knowledge around wealth and abundance. The flow of money and your sense of value and self-worth could increase and fast.

This is the start of the new air era, as the planets Uranus and Pluto are moving into air signs: Uranus into Gemini and Pluto into Aquarius. These air signs represent your money, career and ambition sectors, so this is a significant shift for you. If you're a typical Sun Taurus, you can be resistant to change. Yet the stars are calling you to do things differently, to keep up to date with modern trends and to be one step ahead of the rest of the pack. This could be the year you become an inventor, take a business online or invest in the latest smartphone or laptop. One way or another, it's all about the new.

Pluto, the slowest-moving planet, which spends almost two

decades in one star sign, moved into Aquarius in 2023/2024. As Aquarius is linked to your status and reputation, it's likely that your situation is not going to remain the same moving forward. Perhaps, you're looking towards retirement. Or you're gearing up to step into a position of power and influence. It can work either way. You might take redundancy or be caught up in a situation linked to corruption or wrong-doing. Ready or not, you're being pulled into the new era. You may get a sense of what this will mean for you during Aquarius season, which runs from 19 January to 18 February.

On 30 January and 3 February, the Sun and talk planet Mercury are moving through Aquarius and both make powerful connections with Jupiter in Gemini, linking your money (Gemini) and career (Aquarius) sectors. Put Jupiter, the planet of optimism and faith, in your money sector and these combinations are great for risk-taking. Knowledge is key to your success as the air signs, Gemini and Aquarius, are curious and keen to learn something new.

The air signs are logical and rational and you're a down-to-earth earth sign – you call a spade a spade. Yet this is the year to be open to your spirit guides, your inner voice, a different kind of revelation and awakening. You could be ready to make a leap of faith when Jupiter teams up with the inner planets moving through Aries and the most intuitive sector of your horoscope. The dates to note are 6 April, 5 May and 5 June. These are potentially lucky dates for you, so use them well.

There's also a powerful conjunction between Mercury and Jupiter in Gemini on 8 June. The combination of Mercury and Jupiter is great for meetings, negotiations and new ideas to boost your wealth. Jupiter is a cosmic reminder that luck is an attitude. Sit back and do nothing and luck may not find you.

Have a big vision, be willing to take a risk and have invincible self-belief, then you can fly high. Perhaps now is the time to go on a money mindset course, engage with a new form of learning around finances and investments, and become a more savvy thinker.

Jupiter leaves Gemini on 9 June but there's another important planet entering Gemini on 7 July and that planet is innovative Uranus. Uranus will remain in Gemini until 8 November and returns to Gemini next year on 26 April 2026. Then, Uranus will be bringing its electric energy to your finances for the subsequent seven years. You may get a sense of what this is about for you as soon as Uranus enters Gemini. This is because your ruling planet Venus will be Gemini from 4 July to 31 July. What's beginning in July? What new innovations, inventions or catalysts are emerging?

August may prove significant too. This is when Uranus teams up with two key planets in Aries: Saturn and Neptune. There's a Saturn–Uranus connection on 12 August and a Uranus–Neptune connection on 29 August. This links your past with your future. It may be connected to the cycle of karma and the work you've put in previously to provide for your future financial security. It's also a reminder to trust your instincts, which are a natural part of your earth sign archetype. When you can connect with your inner knowingness, you instinctually make the right moves.

However, it is important to note that Uranus in Gemini doesn't indicate financial stability. Instead, it often coincides with the highs and lows of life, triggering big wins but potentially losses too. You may need to develop a robust risk-taking attitude if you're to do well moving forward.

One way or another, there's a revolution going on within

your finances which may be linked to what's happening within your career or your future path. Don't ignore the winds of change as they are calling to you loudly throughout 2025.

COMMUNITY AND CONNECTIONS

Jupiter moves into water sign Cancer on 9 June beginning a new year-long chapter, as Jupiter will remain here until 30 June 2026. Cancer rules communication and community in your horoscope. This is ideal for all forms of communication, debating, gathering and sharing ideas and information, making new friends and learning new skills. Use your voice to the best of your ability because this could be the start of something big. Jupiter's move through your communication sector could elevate your voice to a new level.

What's important is to decide how you want to actively use Jupiter in your communication, learning and ideas sector. You could go back to school or become a teacher. Alternatively, you may play a significant role within your community or local neighbourhood. Jupiter in Cancer is great for trading, having a market stall and using your voice to win over other people. As Cancer is one of the water signs, this planet/sign combination is caring and compassionate – Jupiter's the great protector and Cancer has a loving nature. A new role as a counsellor perhaps? Or winner of the best neighbour award or community garden?

Cancer rules your siblings and relatives and is the star sign linked to the clan. People power is where it's at and the more you favour your connections, the better.

Two stand-out dates are 24 June and 12 August, when the

Sun and your ruling planet Venus sit next to Jupiter in Cancer. These would be ideal dates to choose to bring people together, to have a reunion or throw a social event close to home.

Once Jupiter's established in Cancer, there are a host of lovely and supportive Jupiter connections to the faster-moving planets in Virgo, a fellow earth sign. Key dates are 22 June, 12 September and 8 October. Virgo is the star sign that rules children in your life and you may be making new connections via your own children or other people's children. Perhaps this is the year you become a godparent, an aunty or uncle, or you start out on a new path as a foster parent. Virgo is the star sign linked to pets too, so it could be an animal sanctuary that has your name on it.

Jupiter in Cancer continues its feel-good journey towards the end of the year. This is when there are lucky encounters between planets in Scorpio and Jupiter in Cancer. The key dates are 24 October, 28 October, 17 November, 26 November and 6 December. These would be excellent dates for starting joint ventures or teaming up in a professional partnership. Scorpio is your opposite star sign so good fortune could come via a third party.

As Jupiter's involved, this feels entrepreneurial and is positive for taking a leap of faith and exploring new business or community connections.

There is one key period in the year when you may have to face a personal challenge and this is 15 June to 19 June. On these dates, Jupiter in Cancer squares up to Saturn and Neptune in Aries and the most private sector of your horoscope. When Saturn and Neptune are working together, feelings of guilt or fear can kick in. For example, you may doubt your ability to help and nurture others. Or you can't let go of the past and this impacts your ability to create a new loving future for yourself.

Jupiter is a planet that favours freedom whereas Saturn and Neptune can reveal where you feel trapped or bound to life. Be honest with yourself if there's something holding you back during this period in the year. If it's a personal issue, what can you do to release its spell upon you? Perhaps this is your opportunity to reach out and ask for the help and support that you need.

Plus, there's been a lot going on in your home and family sector since 2023. And, this year, the stop-start energy continues. On 6 December 2024, action planet Mars turned retrograde in Leo, your home and family sector. Mars is moving back through Leo as 2025 begins. So what's not working out at home or within your family as the year commences? Where are you needing to make adjustments or rethink your options or your next steps?

Mars turns direct on 24 February and will be strong in Leo from 18 April to 17 June. This is a good time to be proactive around renovations, DIY or property transactions. Also this year, communication planet Mercury spends an unusually long time in Leo, from 29 June to 2 September. Mercury in Leo is ideal for heart-to-hearts with loved ones or planning a family get-together, visits or trips away. Mercury is the negotiating planet and so wherever you find Mercury, it's time to talk.

However, Mercury will also be retrograde in Leo from 18 July to 11 August. Perhaps, you're working on your family tree or taking a trip down memory lane. If any misunderstandings arise, wait until mid-August before trying to sort things out. This is when new information may come to light.

This leads you nicely into Venus's journey through Leo from 25 August to 19 September. As Venus is one of the two best planets and your ruling planet, this is an ideal time to heal a rift, invest in property or spend quality time with the ones you love.

FRIENDS AND SOCIETY

There's a lot of planetary activity in Pisces in 2025. Water signs – Cancer, Scorpio, Pisces – represent emotions and they link the people sectors of your horoscope. Therefore, you know straightaway that this is going to be a big year for you when it comes to people and connections.

Pisces represents your friends, groups, associations and your role within society. It's about your hopes and wishes, your place in the world, and the activities and organisations you get involved with. Pisces is an emotional water sign, sensitive and compassionate. It's about the collective unconscious and favours unity rather than division. This means that collaborative ventures rather than competitive alliances are the way forward.

It's important to consider why community, politics, environmental and humanitarian concerns are more important for you now. This sector of your horoscope has been active recently because two major planets, Saturn and Neptune, have been in Pisces in recent years. Neptune's been here since 2012 and Saturn since March 2023.

This year, Saturn remains in Pisces up until 25 May and returns on 1 September. Neptune is here up until 30 March and returns to Pisces on 22 October. Saturn is the planet of authority and responsibility. You may have stepped into a leadership role within a group of people in your life. Alternatively, your political or social allegiances have been tested. Neptune's nature is the opposite of Saturn's; whereas Saturn favours boundaries, limitation and rules, Neptune is a boundless and empathic influence. When these two planets are active in one sector of your horoscope, ideally you want to use them to complement one another. At its best, this combination is a symbol of compassionate idealism. Yet you are a Sun Taurus and one of the fixed signs. When it comes to ideologies, you tend to have rigid or inflexible opinions and don't sway easily. Holding on to your beliefs could get you into trouble this year if you're not prepared to be more tolerant or go with the flow.

There is an unusual amount of planetary activity in Pisces from January through to April. In fact, this period is awash with emotions and there are numerous reasons for this. Firstly, the North Node enters Pisces on 12 January, where it remains until 26 July 2026. The nodes are linked to a call of destiny that you can't avoid and this falls in your friendship sector. Why are you being called to unite with your friends? Perhaps you find your tribe, a spiritual group that feels like home. Pisces is linked to music, art and drugs. You could become a gong bath devotee, start a community art collective or experiment with psychedelic drugs, which are becoming mainstream under Pisces' gaze.

Yet, be wary of being drawn into a cult or losing yourself because of your connection with a group of friends. Keep your earthy common sense intact and your feet firmly planted on the ground. Also, the inner planets Mercury and Venus are in Pisces for some of the time during their retrograde phases. Mercury is retrograde from 15 March to 7 April and Venus is retrograde from 2 March to 13 April. Be wary around friendships during these dates, as retrograde periods can coincide with misunderstandings or misinformation.

Communication planet Mercury and the planet of relating Venus spend longer than usual in Pisces in the first few months of the year. The two planets working together are a social influence. They both interact with the North Node, Saturn and Neptune in Pisces and your friendship and group sector numerous times. This is where there's a flow of energy but it's not always easy. Notice who you're drawn towards, who's a positive influence and who you're wise to steer away from.

To add to the mix of influence in this sector of your horoscope, this year's eclipse cycle is cutting across the Virgo/Pisces axis of the zodiac. The most powerful eclipses for social change and friendship dramas are the Full Moon lunar eclipse in Virgo on 14 March, the New Moon solar eclipse in Pisces on 29 March and the Full Moon lunar eclipse in Pisces on 7 September.

Eclipses are game changers as the wheel of fortune turns and the unexpected occurs. Whatever happens on or around these key dates, wait for the shadow of the eclipse to lift to see what's revealed. You may have a clearer sense of where your alliances and allegiances lie. Also, who you might be up against.

Perhaps, you're campaigning for a political party or singing the praises of a new religion. There may be times you feel swayed as your emotions pull you back and forth. Yet, if you're prepared to open your heart, this could be one of the most connecting and profound years of your life.

KARMA AND INNER WORK

Saturn and Neptune make an important shift this year as they enter a new star sign. These two major planets are heading for an epic conjunction in Aries in February 2026, for the first time since 1989. You're likely to feel the first wave of this as both planets enter fire sign Aries this year. Saturn's in Aries from 25 May to 1 September and Neptune arrives in Aries on 30 March and stays until 22 October. Saturn's journey through Aries will continue next year from 14 February 2026 to April 2028.

Saturn is the more important of the two for you as it's one of the traditional planets. It changes star signs approximately every two years and wherever you find Saturn in your horoscope, this is where commitment and dedication are often required. Also, it's where you find hardship or obstacles in your life. Aries is the most hidden sector of your horoscope, the star sign before yours. It's the place where you're less interested in the ego and more in tune with the spiritual nature of life. You may feel more in flow with the universe and the continual cycle of the Sun, Moon and stars. Perhaps this is the year you become an avid stargazer. Your journey of exploration could take you deep into the psyche or out into the cosmos and the metaphysical realm. Go on a journey of discovery. This is an ideal time in your life for inner work, healing or studying esoteric knowledge.

In June, July and August, when Saturn and Neptune are side by side, you may be seeking both a deeper connection to yourself and to the universe. Also, you might be questioning what gives you meaning in life. This could be a spiritual path or coming home to yourself. You're likely to appreciate rest and retreat, quiet and solitude more than usual.

Saturn in Aries links to your past, even past lives. This could be about your secrets or confidences, your personal issues or hidden affairs. It might coincide with a time when you write your memoirs. Or you're keen to retreat to take on a course of study or commit to a period of research.

Sometimes you have to do your duty when Saturn moves through Aries. You may be caring for a parent or you have other responsibilities that could weigh heavy.

Your ruling planet Venus is leading the way in this new phase and is intimately connected with what's happening. This is because Venus is in Aries not once but twice this year and this is an easier influence. Venus is in Aries from 4 February to 27 March and again from 30 April to 6 June. During these months, you may receive a gift or help from a benefactor. Perhaps a favour is repaid or, you step into a role as a philanthropist or patron.

The Aries/Libra axis of the zodiac has been triggered recently because of the eclipse cycle here. This began in April 2023 and completes on 29 March, when there's a New Moon solar eclipse in Aries. This axis of the zodiac is about health and well-being, also service and sacrifice. Eclipses can act as a wake-up call too. This eclipse falls while two planets are retrograde, Mercury and Venus. Therefore, this would be an ideal time to go on retreat, take time out and prioritise your health. It's important to consider that your well-being is closely connected to your inner process. In other words, take good care of your body and think holistically. Tend to the mind-body-spirit connection.

The last sector of the horoscope is linked to the cycle of karma. And this is where you find Chiron, the wounded healer. Key dates for you may be 12 April, 7 May and 1 June, if you are to release emotions or heal past wounds. Alternatively, you may fall back into old patterns or old ways that no longer serve you. It can be a soul-searching period when planets move through Aries. It could be a powerful time of forgiveness – perhaps of past grievances or in the sense of learning to forgive and love yourself fully.

You may need more time to yourself this year, because of what's happening in your career or out in the world. Perhaps you increasingly want to keep your public life and your personal life separate. With so much activity in Aries this year, you may need more privacy, both online and offline. Ensure you have a place you can escape to, away from the noise and other intrusions.

A SLOWER PACE

Approximately every eighteen months, your ruling planet Venus turns retrograde. Venus spends forty days and forty nights in its retrograde phase, when it disappears from view in the night sky. Before turning retrograde, Venus is an evening star and it reappears as a morning star after its journey of discovery. There are hidden riches to be found when Venus walks on the wild side during its retrograde phase and re-emerges as warrior. This is important to know because Venus will once again journey into the underworld in 2025.

On 4 February, Venus, the planet of relating, enters Aries and turns retrograde in this hidden area of your horoscope on 2 March. Venus will remain on go slow until 13 April. This is a significant retrograde phase for you. Traditionally, the Venus retrograde phase is not the time to engage with Venusian pursuits – i.e. don't marry, have cosmetic surgery or make a major investment, as you may regret your decision or choice once Venus is back up to speed. Sometimes, when Venus is retrograde, you go back to an ex or you become involved in an unrequited love affair. This could be amplified when we take into consideration that it will be in retrograde in Aries, the sector of secrets in your horoscope.

Alternatively, and potentially more productively, you could choose to spend more time on your own with the focus on your inner life. The conversations you have with yourself during this period may be the most revealing and meaningful. In fact, the Venus's retrograde phase could be an important period of soul-searching. This may be your cue to seek insight, either by talking to a counsellor or visiting a healer. Look after yourself and nurture the mind-body-spirit connection.

Above all, Venus's retrograde phase is a time to be reflective and contemplative about love. You may be apart from someone close or experience silence from a loved one. Try to use this phase to take a step back and learn to love yourself most of all.

The pivotal turning point comes on 23 March when the Sun and Venus unite in Aries – a passionate union. The Sun brings light, so themes of illumination and enlightenment are fore-ground. This date could prove to be an important moment for a love relationship. Or for your own self-understanding and insight around love and what it means to you.

After the powerful conjunction with the Sun, Venus starts to gain strength. Venus brings wisdom and experience, once it emerges from the dark and into the light. When it turns direct on 13 April, you may get a better idea about what someone else wants and, most importantly, what you want.

Know that there's no rush leading into 2025 as all three inner planets, Mars, Mercury and Venus, will be retrograde at some point until mid-April. Your ruling planet Venus is the last planet to turn direct. So be mindful and live consciously in the present moving into 2025. Venus is teaching you to savour the small things, to be indulgent and step into the flow of nature. Return to the basics of life and what truly matters the most.

LOVE AND REVELATION

Since 2018, the planet of change, Uranus, has been in Taurus. Uranus is the planet linked to shocks and surprises. Perhaps you've been leading a nomadic or alternative lifestyle, as life is rarely steady and stable when Uranus is in your star sign. This year, Uranus is in your star sign up until 7 July and from 8 November onwards. Then, on 26 April 2026, Uranus will be leaving Taurus and won't be back for another eighty years.

As Uranus has been moving through Taurus, it's been triggering your opposite star sign, Scorpio, and your relationship sector. The radical planet signifies not only personal change but change to your relationship situation too. When it comes to love, Uranus represents the twists and turns of life, the unconventional relationship or the sudden divorce. Alternatively, you fall head over heels in love and love changes everything.

If you were born in the last few days of Taurus season, 18 May to 20 May, you'll be experiencing Uranus's wild planetary energy more powerfully this year. Yet, Uranus leaving your star sign will impact every Taurus and you may be more acutely aware of its influence, as often happens when a planet is moving into or leaving your star sign.

Uranus's radical energy is most intense in your birthday month during the Full Moon phase on 12 May, and also on 17 May and 24 May. Then, on 4 July, it's the annual Venus–Uranus conjunction in your star sign, a significant trigger as Uranus sits next to your ruling planet.

Things can happen quickly when Uranus kicks in and meeting someone new could turn your life on its head. Uranus is the planet linked to technology, so you might meet someone new on an online dating site, who immediately lights up your life.

Yet, what if you're in a relationship or married? Will Uranus spring surprises? It's possible but what's imperative and where the stars can guide you is not to take love for granted. Actively engage with your relationships to keep love fresh and alive. Bring something new to the mix, be spontaneous and loving.

This year's eclipses focus on love too, especially new romance and love affairs. The Full Moon lunar eclipse on 14 March falls in Virgo and your romance sector. Listen carefully to your emotions during the eclipse. Ideally, wait a few days after the eclipse before making any important decisions. Trust your instincts and tap into your natural earthy intuition.

Later in the year, there are not one but two New Moons in Virgo and this is unusual. A New Moon is a symbol of new beginnings. The first takes place on 23 August, an excellent date to set your intentions around fun and pleasure, children and romance. The second New Moon in Virgo is a solar eclipse on 21 September, the day before the equinox. A New Moon solar eclipse is a power point of energy and there could be good reason to celebrate on or around this date.

Your ruling planet Venus is in Virgo too from 19 September to 13 October. Therefore, things could happen fast in the areas of romance and pleasure during this period. Fast forward to November and Venus moves into Scorpio and your relationship sector from 6 November to 30 November. This may be an especially lively period for your love life.

However, talk planet Mercury is retrograde from 9 November to 29 November. For some of this retrograde phase, Mercury is in Scorpio and your relationship sector. Things can be hidden from you when Mercury's on go slow. Or perhaps someone goes quiet on you. Whatever intrigues are playing out, wait until Mercury turns direct to reopen the lines of communication.

This is often a time when new information or the truth comes to light.

In addition, Jupiter and Uranus are both active during the last months of the year and both planets are important when it comes to love. Jupiter is a positive influence as it teams up with the inner planets in Scorpio, encouraging love and relationships to grow, flourish and prosper. The key dates are 24 October, 28 October, 17 November, 22 November, 26 November and 6 December. Yet, Uranus is bringing something new and unexpected to the mix as it opposes the inner planets in Scorpio and your relationship sector. The key dates are 19 November, 21 November, 30 November and 10 December.

You may be willing to take more risks than usual at the end of the year and both Jupiter and Uranus have a theme of freedom and doing what's right for you. It's potentially an intense period for love when the planets are encouraging you to do things differently and embrace change.

RULING PLANET

Knowing where your ruling planet Venus is in your horoscope can help you plan ahead. Venus is the planet of attraction, popularity and pleasure. Which areas of your life does Venus light up? Here's the pattern:

Up until 3 January: Venus in Aquarius – career and vocation

3 January to 4 February: Venus in Pisces – friendship and groups

4 February to 27 March: Venus in Aries – hidden sector – retreat, rest, inner work

27 March to 30 April: Venus in Pisces – friendship and groups

30 April to 6 June: Venus in Aries – hidden sector – retreat, rest, inner work

6 June to 4 July: Venus in Taurus – your personal goals and aims, image and profile

4 July to 31 July: Venus in Gemini – money matters

31 July to 25 August: Venus in Cancer – community and communication

25 August to 19 September: Venus in Leo – home and family, your past

19 September to 13 October: Venus in Virgo – romance, creativity, children, fun

13 October to 6 November: Venus in Libra – work and lifestyle

6 November to 30 November: Venus in Scorpio – relationships and contracts

30 November to 24 December: Venus in Sagittarius – joint finances and shared resources

24 December onwards: Venus in Capricorn – travel and study, the bigger picture

LUCKY DATES

Venus turns direct – 13 April

Your New Moon Taurus – new beginnings – 27 April

Venus Aries sextile Jupiter Gemini – 5 June

Venus conjunct Uranus Taurus – 4 July

Venus conjunct Jupiter Cancer – 12 August

Venus Virgo sextile Jupiter Cancer – 8 October

Your Full Moon Taurus – achievement/culmination – 5 November

Venus Scorpio trine Jupiter Cancer – 26 November

GEMINI

YOUR 2025 HOROSCOPE

GEMINI RULERSHIPS

ZODIAC SYMBOL: THE TWINS

RULING PLANET: MERCURY,
THE COMMUNICATOR

MODE/ELEMENT: MUTABLE AIR –
FLIGHTY, VERSATILE, QUICK-WITTED,
MISCHIEVOUS

COLOUR: YELLOW, MULTI-COLOURED

ARCHETYPE: THE MESSENGER,
THE TRICKSTER

YOUR TOP TIPS FOR 2025

EMBRACE FREEDOM, START A
GROUNDBREAKING STUDY COURSE

FIND YOUR CREATIVE MUSE,
FOLLOW YOUR TRUE VOCATION

CREATE A FINANCIAL PORTFOLIO,
BOOST YOUR FAMILY'S FORTUNES

HANG OUT WITH THE RIGHT KIND OF
FRIENDS AND MAKE ALLIANCES

LEARN TO SWITCH OFF YOUR BUSY MIND

Ⅱ

NEW BEGINNINGS

The year starts with some big news, which is that the planet of luck, opportunity and good fortune, Jupiter, is moving through your star sign. Jupiter entered Gemini on 25 May 2024, where it remains until 9 June 2025. This major event only happens once every twelve years, so make the most of it. Wherever Jupiter goes, opportunity follows. While Jupiter's in your star sign, turn your attention towards your personal goals and aims, your image and profile. Take care of your body and well-being too.

When Jupiter's in full flow, you want to see the world and save the world. What's not advised when Jupiter's prominent in your horoscope is to play small or stay at home. Jupiter rewards bold behaviour and loves the free spirit, the explorer, the entrepreneur, the lover of life. Anything that begins under Jupiter's rule promises success. Jupiter's a reminder that luck is an attitude. When you have a big vision, a willingness to take risks and believe in yourself and what you're doing, this is when you attract good fortune.

Jupiter rules travel, education, religion, philosophy and philan-thropy. It's the planet connected to publishing and the law, also foreign connections. This might be the year you flex your Gemini skills and become a translator, a linguist or journalist. Your star sign is ruled by Mercury, the fleet-footed messenger and the planet of communication. You make a natural trader and salesperson with your gift of the gab.

Your ruling planet, Mercury, is in Gemini from 26 May to 8 June. This is when you may gain a confidence boost or your energy levels will be high, peaking with the final connection between Mercury and Jupiter, before they change star sign – the stand-out date while Jupiter's in Gemini is 8 June, the day when your ruling planet, Mercury, teams up with Jupiter in your star sign. These two planets work well together. They're both linked to education, movement and travel. There may be good news or you're celebrating a win or achievement. This date falls right at the end of Jupiter's journey through your star sign. Therefore, consider what you're working towards and what you want to achieve by the middle of the year. Think of yourself as a magician when Mercury and Jupiter come together. What are you conjuring up, where are you bringing hope and faith into the mix?

There are other times in the year that it's worth making the most of Jupiter's bounty. On 30 January and 3 February, Jupiter in Gemini aligns with planets in Aquarius and your travel and study sector. You're being encouraged to open up your world and live life to the full.

Fast forward to 6 April, 5 May and 5 June, and Jupiter in Gemini aligns with planets in Aries and your friendship and group sector. Together, you're bigger and better. Find your tribe – arrange a holiday with friends or join a group study course. The only proviso is that your planet Mercury is retrograde from 15 March to 7 April. This can be a time of communication chaos when things don't work out the way you want them to. However, Mercury retrograde phases are ideal for all the 're'-words –

reviewing, reflecting, retreating, reconsidering. Turn inward while Mercury's on go slow and consider your options carefully.

Even though Jupiter leaves your star sign on 9 June, that doesn't mean there's nothing else going on here. In fact, this year you have a major event taking place in your star sign, Gemini. This is the arrival of the planet Uranus in Gemini for the first time in over eighty years. Uranus enters your star sign on 7 July where it remains until 8 November. Then, Uranus will return to Gemini on 26 April 2026, where it stays for the following seven years.

Uranus is the planet linked to unpredictability, surprises and change. If you're ready for a revolution in your life or you can sense your inner rebel wanting to grab life by the reins, here's your opportunity. Uranus represents a lightning bolt and your star sign is mutable and flexible. You're likely to be more restless during this period and you may have to embrace change, ready or not. Uranus rules science, technology, innovation, invention, the modern age and all things new. So the message is clear: don't stay stuck in a rut but embrace progress and keep moving your life forward. Be a rebel or an activist and stand up for what you believe in. You can be a powerful voice of change in your own and other people's lives. Notice what's awakening inside you and where you want to do things differently or step up and play your part within society.

Uranus can be an erratic influence too. You might choose to turn off the news or take a digital detox and seek balance or calm in your life. If you're a typical Gemini, you overthink things because you have a busy mind. It may become more urgent to silence the noise. The Mercury retrograde phase in the middle of the year – 18 July to 11 August – would be an ideal time to take a step back. Mercury is retrograde in Leo and your communication sector. This would be an ideal time to go on retreat, be silent or chill out on holiday.

August may be when you start to recognise how Uranus in Gemini is going to revolutionise or awaken your life. On 12 August and 29 August, Uranus teams up with key planets Saturn and Neptune in Aries, which is your friendship and group sector. Therefore, this is a time when you may be at the forefront of an organisation. Or you may be ready to be the voice or mouthpiece for an association, political party or good cause. During this period in the year, it's wise to ask what's calling you and where can you use your unique skills to benefit society.

Take hold of the reins of excitement and innovation. This isn't a time to hold steady and resist change. Instead, keep moving forward, sometimes with little steps and other times with a huge leap. Stake your claim and find your voice in the new age.

MONEY AND INVESTMENT

You're heading into an easier phase financially in 2025. For example, you no longer have the slowest-moving planet Pluto in Capricorn and your joint finance sector. Pluto moved here in 2008, which coincided with a global financial crash, and finally left Capricorn in 2023/2024.

Pluto can be a tough archetype as it's linked to loss, debt and corruption. You may have experienced your own Pluto-influenced experiences. At its most extreme, this could mean bankruptcy or racking up debt. Alternatively, you may have been obsessively involved with money. Perhaps, you became a 'plutocrat' or you've invested successfully in assets and property.

Pluto is the planet of power and transformation, as well as loss.

Either way, Pluto is no longer in your joint finance sector and there's fresh energy sweeping in. Though this may not be evident straight away. As the year begins, action planet Mars is retrograde and moves back into Cancer and your personal money sector on 6 January. Mars first entered Cancer from 4 September to 4 November 2024. Then, Mars turned retrograde on 6 December 2024 and returns to Cancer at the start of this year. Perhaps it's been a disruptive period for finances with more expense than usual or more money going out than coming in. When Mars is retrograde, you're wise to take your foot off the money accelerator. Slow things down and don't make a wrong move. You don't want to end up running in the wrong direction financially.

The turning point comes on 24 February when Mars turns direct. Use this date to be assertive and push things through. Chase up outstanding payments and be proactive when it comes to finances.

Mars is in Cancer and your personal money sector until 18 April, so make the most of this. It's a positive period in the year in which to get things moving. Cancer not only rules money in your horoscope, but also your assets and possessions. And it's linked to your values and self-worth. There's strong focus on your values and what matters to you most. This could stem from your financial circumstances. Or perhaps you're starting to become more aware of how your success is closely aligned with your self-worth. Cancer is the star sign of the home and family, which means this isn't only about getting your finances sorted but your loved one's finances too.

The big news is that, on 9 June, Jupiter leaves your star sign and enters Cancer, where it remains until 30 June 2026. While

Jupiter's in Cancer, seek new opportunities to boost your finances so you can lead a wealthier or more abundant lifestyle. Jupiter's the planet of good fortune and plenty. You may be in a position to pay off debt or be able to boost your financial future, for yourself and your family.

Jupiter is also linked to truth and justice. Therefore, this may spell good news if you're fighting a legal case or you're on a mission to expose corruption or wrong-doing. Jupiter in Cancer is a protective influence, so you may take on a protective role within your family, both financially and emotionally. Or, you realise there's more benefit in joining forces and teaming up with other people.

This year, there are two major conjunctions in Cancer between the Sun and Jupiter on 24 June and Venus and Jupiter on 12 August. The Sun illuminates and Venus is linked to love and money.

These combinations promise good fortune and you may receive a gift or bonus. Perhaps, you set up a part-time business working from home. Or you join a company that has a strong policy of family ethics and caring for its employees.

There are some lucky aspects between Jupiter and the inner planets in Virgo and your home and family sector. These take place on 22 June, 12 September and 8 October. Invest money in your home or look at ways of earning money through your property. This could include renting out a room, setting yourself up as a film location or holding a garage sale at home.

A key period to be cautious around money is 15 June to 19 June, when Jupiter in Cancer clashes with Saturn and Neptune in Aries and your friendship and group sector. Be careful what you get involved in during this period as it could cost you dearly. It's not the best time to put money into a group or association or mix money and friendship.

Towards the end of the year, Jupiter teams up with planets in Scorpio on 24 October, 28 October, 17 November, 22 November, 26 November and 6 December. Scorpio rules your work and your health. Therefore, these are the key areas of your life in which new opportunities could arise and you're being encouraged to invest wisely. The only proviso is that your ruling planet Mercury is retrograde from 9 November to 29 November. This is a positive period to review your situation but not to make any major investments or major decisions. Instead, wait until Mercury turns direct to sign and seal a work contract or accept a new job.

Use Jupiter's influence well this year and put more energy and enthusiasm into attracting wealth and abundance into your life.

CAREER AND DESTINY

Since March 2023, Saturn has been in Pisces and your career and vocation sector. Saturn is the planet of authority and discipline, endings, hard work and commitment. Also, there's been another powerful influence in this sector of your horoscope in the shape of Neptune. Neptune is the planet of dreams and imagination, but also disillusionment and fantasy. Neptune's one of the slower-moving planets and has been in Pisces since 2012. This year, there's a major shift as both planets start to move out of Pisces. Therefore, this may be a transitional year for you career-wise, with a possible ending on the horizon, but also new inspiration or opportunities.

As a flighty Gemini, Saturn in your career and vocation sector can benefit you and keep you on track with your long-term goals. Saturn turns dreams into reality, so it signifies a time to get serious about where you're heading and why. However, Saturn isn't always an easy influence as it's the planet of hardship, limits and obstacles. Perhaps, you've been working overly hard for little reward. Or you've been unemployed or feel lost and confused about your next steps. While Pisces rules your status and reputation too, and there's a possibility that your reputation may have been damaged over the last couple of years. All this could begin to change as Saturn moves out of Pisces this year, from 25 May to 1 September, and Neptune moves out of Pisces from 30 March to 22 October. Next year, Saturn will exit Pisces on 14 February and Neptune on 26 January 2026. The tides are turning as a new chapter begins to unfold.

This may be something you become aware of early in the year as your ruling planet Mercury spends an unusually long time in your career and future sector. Mercury's in Pisces from 14 February to 3 March and again from 30 March to 16 April. This tells you that Mercury is turning retrograde and will be on go slow from 15 March to 7 April. Don't make any key decisions or major investments while Mercury's retrograde. Instead, go back over old ground, review your options and keep an open mind.

The beginning of the year is powerful for other reasons. Firstly, the North Node enters Pisces on 12 January, where it remains until 26 July 2026. The nodes are linked to a call of destiny that you can't avoid and they're moving through your career and future sector.

Secondly, the planet of relating, Venus, is in Pisces from 3 January to 4 February, and again from 27 March to 30 April. In addition to Mercury retrograde, there's a Venus retrograde phase from 2 March to 13 April. Having both planets retrograde at the same time means that you may lose someone's support.

Or career plans that were in discussion are put on hold. This adds to the soul-searching theme of the first few months of 2025. If you're unhappy or discontent with your current path, this could overwhelm you from January through to April.

What the stars are calling you to do is to surrender to the unknown. See where life takes you but don't make any final decision until mid-April.

Sometimes, retrograde phases can be revealing and a powerful creative source. Pisces is a star sign that's linked to music, art, poetry and spirituality. And it's a compassionate influence. So if you follow your destiny early this year, you could end up pursuing an artistic or spiritual path. Or you say yes to a career or vocation where you're doing good in the world.

This year's eclipse cycle is powerful too as it cuts across the Virgo/Pisces axis of the zodiac and the foundations of your life. Sometimes during eclipses, one door has to close before a new door can open. They are often linked to new beginnings that follow on from an ending. Looking back, they often coincide with key turning points in your life. The current Virgo/Pisces eclipse cycle began in September 2024 and completes in February 2027. The last time you had this same eclipse cycle was 18–19 years ago.

There are two Full Moon lunar eclipses this year: the first on 14 March and the second on 7 September. These periods in the year could bring some challenges your way, perhaps the end of a chapter. Yet they can be powerful pointers in a new direction, when you're able to take advantage of change. Perhaps you realise that your work/life balance is out. Or you feel off track and non-aligned with your destiny. Alternatively, you could be promoted or step into a new position of responsibility. Eclipses represent accelerated growth, as the wheel of fortune speeds up.

There is another important factor this year – the emphasis on the air signs, your element. Air represents networks, information highways, communication and connections, technology and ideas. Your natural ability as a communicator is likely to be in demand in this new era.

In 2023/2024, power planet Pluto moved into your fellow air sign Aquarius, linked to travel and study, the bigger picture of life. Aquarius is the star sign linked to humanitarian, environmental and social concerns and rules the collective. You may step into a position of power within society. Or have a burning desire to focus on sustainability in business or set up a community collective that brings people together. You might be at the forefront of new technologies, such as AI, ensuring that rules and regulations are put in place to stop the theft of people's work across the internet.

You have a clever mind, being a Sun Gemini. Consider how you can use your brain and communication skills in a way that furthers progress. Keep your eyes firmly fixed on the future in 2025 and beyond.

FRIENDS AND GROUPS

When the planets Saturn and Neptune leave Pisces, they move into Aries, the star sign ruling your friends and group associations. Saturn is in Aries from 25 May to 1 September, and Neptune is here from 30 March to 22 October. Aries represents any club, group or society you belong to, whether political, social, humanitarian or environmental. It's where you find your tribe and connect with people of like minds.

The most important planet of the two is Saturn, as it's one

of the traditional planets and represents authority, duty and responsibility. If you're a typical Gemini, these attributes are to be learned through life, as they're not always given at birth. Therefore, wherever you find Saturn in your horoscope, things can weigh heavy. If you're asked to take on a role of responsibility while Saturn's in Aries, question your motivations. You may be stepping up through a sense of guilt or fear, or feel pressured into taking on a role that you don't really want. A group association could come to an end when Saturn moves into Aries. Or your interest wanes and you realise it's the right time to move on.

Favour honest friendships in your life, especially in June, July and August, and keep clear boundaries in place. Saturn and Neptune are side by side during this period, getting ready for their major conjunction in Aries in February 2026. Saturn and Neptune working together can flag up themes of betrayal or playing victim. Notice where you're being pulled into other people's lives and don't get sucked in by manipulative or unethical behaviour. This may be about your role within the collective. You have a quick mind, being a Gemini, and you can be easily swayed. Try to see both sides of the coin and be wary of ideologies that don't benefit the common good.

Your friendships and group associations may be one of your biggest learnings this year, but this is not necessarily something new. This is because of the recent eclipse cycle cutting across the Aries/Libra axis of the zodiac. This eclipse cycle began in April 2023 and completes in March 2025. There have been two powerful New Moon solar eclipses in Aries in 2023 and 2024, and there's a third and final solar eclipse here on 29 March. You may already have cut ties with one friendship group. Or perhaps a door has closed on your association with a group, club or society. This may have happened in a dramatic or unpleasant manner. What door are you closing during this year's powerful solar eclipse?

Alternatively, someone new may come into your life and make a difference. Your associations have power within them during a solar eclipse. You might be hanging out with friends in high places or have a bestie who's an influencer.

There's another astrological influence in Aries involving retrograde planets. The planet of relating, Venus, turns retrograde in Aries on 2 March and your ruling planet, Mercury, turns retrograde in Aries on 15 March. These two planets are going back and forth in this key area of your life throughout February, March, April and May. This period in the year could be pivotal for you when it comes to your friends and group associations. It's about the people you encounter, both socially and professionally.

Wait for Mercury and Venus to turn direct mid-April before speaking up or confronting someone. During retrograde phases, there's often misunderstandings and miscommunication. If you're a typical Gemini, friends are important to you and you often have a diverse social circle. You don't tend to shy away from conflict either and you may love a good debate. Yet, if there's a falling out with a friend, it can be challenging for you.

Aim to align yourself with the right people this year. March is potentially the trickiest month for your alliances and group associations. Whereas the second half of April and the month of May is a time to start forming new alliances, as well as ensuring firm boundaries are in place.

You can't discount the fact that your friends are going to be a huge influence in your life, not only in 2025 but moving forward. A friend or colleague could step into a prestigious role or become a household name. You may do well to ride their wave of success alongside them.

HOME AND HEALTH

You have a lot of astrology pulling you out into the world in 2025. Yet there are other key areas of your life under the cosmic spotlight. Firstly, the current Virgo/Pisces eclipse cycle highlights not only your career and future path (Pisces), but also your home and family, your roots and your past (Virgo). Virgo is the star sign at the base of your horoscope. When you have eclipses cutting across this powerful axis of the horoscope from the base (Virgo) to the peak (Pisces), it's often a time when you change jobs or move house. Sometimes, the two are linked.

The key areas of home and family, career and future path, are where you may be at a crossroads and where you can expect change and accelerated growth. This particular eclipse cycle runs from September 2024 to February 2027 and peaks in March and September this year.

The Full Moon lunar eclipse on 14 March falls in Virgo, and your home and family sector. You may be making a big decision or have to take responsibility for a parent or someone else in the family on or around this eclipse.

Virgo season takes place later in the year, from 22 August to 22 September. Plus, your ruling planet, Mercury, whizzes through Virgo from 2 September to 18 September. This is when you can make fast progress around the home and family affairs.

And, this year, there are not one but two New Moons in Virgo, a symbol of new beginnings. The first takes place on 23 August, an ideal date to set your intentions around your home and your family. The second takes place on 21 September, the day before the equinox. This is no ordinary New Moon as it's a solar eclipse in Virgo, a power point of energy and the portal to a new era. Seeds that are sown on or around this powerful solar eclipse could transform your home or family life over the next few years. You might be the one making a snap decision that impacts your family. Alternatively, a family member could be leaving home or moving on to a new domestic situation.

Consider what new initiatives may not only benefit you but the ones you love, and embrace the wheels of change as a new phase kicks in. However, it is important to consider your own needs at this time. Notice what you might be giving up by prioritising family and what would benefit you moving forward. If you are moving home or dealing with major family issues, this can take its toll on you personally.

Close to the eclipse date, action planet Mars moves into Scorpio and your health sector on 22 September. And all the inner planets will be moving through this part of your horoscope up until mid-December. This is a period in the year when you're wise to prioritise your health and look after yourself.

In addition, live-wire Uranus moves back into Taurus and the most hidden sector of your horoscope on 8 November. Uranus can be an erratic and unpredictable influence. In Taurus, it turns your attention inward. If you're experiencing too much noise in your life or in your head, prioritise your health and well-being.

Uranus opposes planets in Scorpio on 19 November, 21 November, 30 November and 10 December. Plus, your ruling planet, Mercury, is retrograde from 9 November to 29 November – a double whammy of planetary activity encouraging you to slow down, switch off, rest and retreat. If you can, take some time out during this crazy phase in the year. Alternatively, use the Mercury retrograde phase to explore your health options, read up about new discoveries linked to the mind and look for new and alternative treatments to improve your health and diet.

It's not wise to be impulsive or reckless with your health. Yet, it is a promising time to experiment with something new, even something radical. Your stars are encouraging you to embrace new technologies and innovations to boost your energy levels. You could practise breathwork or experiment with fasting to boost your metabolism. Alternatively, you could go old school and take up tennis or yoga. Or you could put your communication skills to good practice in journalling or counselling. Most importantly, stay mobile and flexible, your Gemini hallmarks.

LOVE AND ROMANCE

When it comes to love, your star sign Gemini is atypical – i.e. anything goes. You have a mercurial nature, being ruled by Mercury, and you're not easily constrained into one classic love archetype. Jupiter is your partner planet. And, with Jupiter in Gemini for the first five months of the year, you're wise to ensure that fun and communication are the main ingredients in any relationship. Your ideal partner is someone who's not only your best friend but makes your life better for being in it.

This year, love and friendship are linked, but not always in easy aspect. Note that both talk planet Mercury and the planet of love Venus spend some time retrograde in your friendship sector during March. Sometimes, when you have key planets retrograde, you reconnect with someone from your past. Or an ex gets back in touch.

Certainly, a friendship could promise passion, especially on or around 23 March, when the Sun and Venus unite in Aries. This can often be a time of deep insight and revelation. Yet you're wise to remain open-minded until Mercury and Venus are back to direct motion mid-April. The key turning point is 13 April when love planet Venus turns direct. This is the same day as a Full Moon in Libra, the star sign linked to relationships. Libra is your romance sector and it would be an ideal time to declare your feelings. If you've been exploring a new relationship, the answer's yes.

Passion planet Mars is moving through Libra from 6 August to 22 September, the start of another potentially exciting period for love. Your planet Mercury is in Libra from 18 September to 6 October, followed by love planet Venus from 13 October to 6 November. Libra rules children as well as romance in your horoscope. This could be a key period in the year for you if you're planning to become a parent.

Venus's move through Sagittarius and your relationship sector is often a time when love peaks in your life. This is from 30 November to 24 December, promising a romantic lead up to the festive season. Also, your ruler Mercury is in Sagittarius from 29 October to 19 November, and again from 11 December onwards. However, this is where Mercury turns retrograde on 9 November and remains on go slow until 29 November.

Whether you're in a relationship or not, the general trend seems to be flexibility, needing space to do your own thing and the freedom to focus on your bigger goals. If you're a typical Gemini, you're changeable and mercurial. Therefore, the ideal relationship for you is one where you're best friends and there's movement and curiosity too.

RULING PLANET

Wherever you find your planet Mercury, this is where you can make quick progress (except for when Mercury is retrograde – see dates above). Use your people skills, your communication abilities, your gift of the gab. Here's the pattern:

Up until 9 January: Mercury in Sagittarius – relationships and contracts

9 January to 28 January: Mercury in Capricorn – joint finances and taboo issues

28 January to 14 February: Mercury in Aquarius – travel and study, the bigger picture

14 February to 3 March: Mercury in Pisces – career and vocation

3 March to 30 March: Mercury in Aries – friendship and groups

30 March to 16 April: Mercury in Pisces – career and vocation

16 April to 10 May: Mercury in Aries – friendship and groups

10 May to 26 May: Mercury in Taurus – hidden sector – retreat, rest, inner work

26 May to 8 June: Mercury in Gemini – your personal goals and aims, image and profile

8 June to 26 July: Mercury in Cancer – money, assets, values

26 June to 2 September: Mercury in Leo – community and communication

2 September to 18 September: Mercury in Virgo – home and family, your past

18 September to 6 October: Mercury in Libra – romance, creativity, children

6 October to 29 October: Mercury in Scorpio – work and health

29 October to 19 November: Mercury in Sagittarius – relationships and contracts

19 November to 11 December: Mercury in Scorpio – work and health

11 December onwards: Mercury in Sagittarius – relationships and contracts

LUCKY DATES

Mercury Aquarius trine Jupiter Gemini – 3 February

Mercury Aries sextile Jupiter Gemini – 5 May

Your New Moon Gemini – new beginnings – 27 May

Mercury conjunct Jupiter Gemini – 8 June

Sun conjunct Jupiter Cancer – 24 June

Venus conjunct Jupiter Cancer – 12 August

Your Full Moon Gemini – achievement/culmination – 4 December

Mercury Scorpio trine Jupiter Cancer – 6 December

CANCER

YOUR 2025 HOROSCOPE

CANCER RULERSHIPS

ZODIAC SYMBOL: THE CRAB

RULING PLANET: MOON, LADY OF THE NIGHT, THE REALM OF SUBCONSCIOUS AND DREAMS

MODE/ELEMENT: CARDINAL WATER – REFLECTIVE, SENTIMENTAL, NURTURING, CARING

COLOUR: SILVER, WHITE

ARCHETYPE: THE MOTHER, THE HUNTRESS – GODDESS OF THE MOON

YOUR TOP TIPS FOR 2025

WRITE YOUR MEMOIRS, FOLLOW YOUR SPIRITUAL CALLING

CARE FOR OTHERS, BECOME A COACH OR COUNSELLOR

TURN A DREAM INTO REALITY, SET UP YOUR OWN BUSINESS

BE INSPIRED BY NEW FRIENDS, HAVE A SEXY LOVE AFFAIR

TRANSFORM YOUR FINANCES, PROTECT YOUR FINANCIAL FUTURE

♋

SELF-IMPROVEMENT
AND SPIRITUALITY

It takes Jupiter twelve years to circuit the zodiac, and so it spends approximately one year in each star sign. The best news for you this year is that Jupiter will enter Cancer on 9 June. Before then, however, Jupiter is completing its journey through Gemini, the previous star sign to yours. This focuses your attention on the most hidden sector of your horoscope – the realm of the subconscious, dreams and spirituality.

If you're a typical Sun Cancer, your emotions will ebb and flow like your ruler the Moon, a changeable shape-shifter. You have a deep emotional life and your inner life can be vivid. Jupiter expands what it touches and while it is in Gemini, your inner life may be extremely busy. Gemini is the sign of communication linked to the mind. If your thoughts are going into overdrive, express your emotions, ideas and dreams through the spoken and written word.

Sometimes when Jupiter's in Gemini, you want or need more time to yourself to rest and retreat, to be quiet and still. Seek solitude when you need it because this is where your most creative ideas could be born.

Jupiter activity peaks on 8 June when there's a major planetary conjunction between communication planet Mercury and

Jupiter. This might be a time when you're researching, studying or writing. Alternatively, you may receive an award or an achievement, linked to study or education, publishing or the law.

Self-care plays a vital role when you have Jupiter in Gemini, so tend your own needs and listen attentively to your inner voice. Become your own best friend. Though caring for others is a key part of Jupiter's journey through this sector of your horoscope too. Jupiter's a protective influence and your star sign Cancer is kind and sensitive.

You may work in a hospice, hospital or prison. You might be reading letters or journals from the past or be delving into history in some other way. You may become a keeper of secrets during this powerful Jupiter transit.

This is the air sign era and Gemini is one of the air signs. There's another powerful planet in air sign Aquarius throughout 2025 and that planet is Pluto, god of the underworld. Pluto was moving in and out of Aquarius through 2023/2024 and it's now taken up residence in Aquarius for the next twenty years. In your horoscope, the air signs connect you with the most private and inner part of yourself, also connections to the past, your legacy and where you come from. You may be more closely aware of the cycle of life, death and rebirth and life beyond the veil while Pluto's in Aquarius. You may read books about near-death experiences, mysteries of the universe or spirituality.

The period from 30 January to 3 February could be pivotal as the inner planets in Aquarius connect with Jupiter in Gemini. Be willing to venture into new places and embrace the unknown, going where others fear to tread. The year 2025 could take you on an inner journey that's fascinating and grabs hold of you one hundred per cent.

There's another influence in Gemini this year, as one of the generational planets Uranus moves into Gemini from 7 July to 8 November. Uranus takes approximately eighty years to circuit the zodiac so this is a rare event. Uranus will return to Gemini next year on 26 April, where it will remain for the following seven years. Uranus in Gemini can be an erratic or unpredictable influence. Therefore, you're wise to counteract this with spiritual disciplines that help calm your mind. Learn to meditate, start your day with a morning journal or listen to hypnotherapy music or spiritual podcasts. Find your own form of prayer. Reach out to other people who are seekers of life, so you feel connected to life.

Uranus represents innovation and invention. Therefore, it's potentially a genius element when Uranus is in Gemini. Don't underestimate the power of your intellect and the brilliance of your ideas. August could be a stand-out month, when new developments or learnings could benefit your career or future path. The dates to note are 12 August and 29 August.

This major journey of Uranus in Gemini coincides with the planet of opportunity, Jupiter, in your star sign, making it an ideal time to expand your horizons and push back the boundaries of life.

SAY YES TO LIFE

A significant date for you this year is 9 June. This is when the luckiest planet Jupiter enters your star sign, where it will remain until 30 June 2026. Wherever Jupiter goes, opportunity and good fortune follow. Therefore, you're wise to make the most of Jupiter in your star sign. Jupiter is a reminder that luck is an attitude – i.e. when you have a big vision, when you're willing to take risks and you have belief in yourself and what you're doing, good fortune follows. It's not a time to sit back and wait for luck to land in your lap. Instead, look to the future and say yes to life. Jupiter in Cancer is an ideal time to be your own cheerleader. This is about your personal goals and aims, your image and profile. Be proud of who you are, know yourself well and do more of what you love.

Jupiter is the planet linked to freedom, encouraging you to let go of ties that bind you and anything or anyone who holds you back. When Jupiter's in full flow, you want to see the world and save the world. Jupiter rules travel, education, spirituality, philosophy and philanthropy. It's the planet of foreign connections, publishing, higher education and the law. What's not advised when Jupiter is in your star sign is to play small. Jupiter rewards bold behaviour and loves the free spirit, the explorer, the entrepreneur, the lover of life. Jupiter rules truth and justice, so be true to your beliefs and be your authentic self.

Do something special to honour Jupiter's move into Cancer, whether that means a big party and celebration. Or perhaps you will take part in a global event – a conference or workshop.

This leads you into Cancer season, when the Sun is in your star sign from 21 June to 22 July and it's your birthday month. The peak dates for activity involving Jupiter in Cancer are 24 June and 12 August. This is when the Sun sits next to Jupiter in Cancer, followed by Venus next to Jupiter in Cancer. The Sun illuminates and is linked to energy and confidence. Venus is the planet of love and money, art and beauty – the second-best planet after Jupiter. Make the most of these stand-out dates in the year and say yes to life.

If you're a typical Sun Cancer, you care deeply about other

people and your loved ones. While Jupiter's in your star sign, it makes some lovely connections with planets in people sectors of your horoscope, bringing out the caring side of your nature. On 22 June, 12 September and 8 October, Jupiter in Cancer teams up with planets in Virgo and your community sector. Meet up with your siblings or relatives, get to know your neighbours better or start a community initiative. These are positive dates in the year to be more involved with your local neighbourhood, in whatever way suits you. You could step into a teaching role or become a volunteer. Do what feels right for you.

Then, on 24 October, 28 October, 17 November, 26 November and 6 December, Jupiter in Cancer teams up with planets in Scorpio, a fellow water sign. Scorpio represents children in your life, also lovers and playmates. If you're a parent, you might celebrate a child's achievement on or around these dates. Or perhaps you're keen to start a family or decide to become a foster parent. Your nurturing, caring nature will expand as Jupiter moves through your star sign.

Jupiter's journey through Cancer is the right time to expand your life and say yes to new opportunities. Astrology enables you to work with the right timing, to know when to be expansive and when to rein things in. This is important to know because, at the start of this year, action planet Mars is retrograde in your star sign from 6 January to 24 February. When Mars is retrograde, you're often caught up in a stop-start scenario and you can't get ahead the way you would like. Sometimes, your energy levels are low or you're lacking motivation.

The turning point comes on 24 February when Mars turns direct in your star sign. Try again where things didn't work out and focus on your next steps. This is a good time to set new resolutions for those next steps.

Mars remains in Cancer until 18 April. This confirms that 2025 is a powerful year to put yourself first and focus on your personal goals and aims. Mars is a physical planet so you might be keen to get fit or boost your health. Strength training would be an ideal fitness activity with Mars in your star sign. Get yourself ready and prepared to make the most of Jupiter's journey through your star sign later in the year.

CAREER AND FUTURE PATH

A major shift takes place this year, as the planet of discipline and hard work, Saturn, enters Aries, the star sign ruling your career and vocation, your status and reputation. Saturn takes approximately thirty years to circuit the zodiac. It will be in Aries from 25 May to 1 September. Saturn returns to Aries next year on 14 February 2026, where it will remain until April 2028. This could coincide with a step up the career ladder, a chance to get serious about work and where you're heading. Saturn is the taskmaster of the heavens, so you're wise to turn your focus to the future and consider how you can achieve your long-term goals.

As Saturn remains in Aries for the best part of three years, this would be the ideal time to draw up a business plan or commit to a long-term work project. Saturn in Aries benefits from good time management, self-discipline, structure and firm foundations. This isn't about achieving overnight success. Instead, it's about planning for the future and proving you can do what you say and stick to your commitments. It's how you go about things that will decide whether this next phase in your life is a success. You may have to develop patience and give up short-term gratification in exchange for long-term achievement. Saturn in Aries could be a fitting symbol for running your own business or becoming your own boss.

Sometimes, when you have Saturn at the peak of your horoscope, a significant chapter in your life is coming to an end. You may be getting ready for retirement, or perhaps you have other responsibilities or duties that demand your attention. This may be linked to your parents or a caretaker role.

There may be times this year when things don't work out easily. For example, talk planet Mercury turns retrograde in Aries on 15 March and remains on go slow until 7 April. When Mercury's retrograde, this isn't the best time to make a major decision or start something new, especially regarding your career or future path. That's not to say you won't hear of something new during the Mercury retrograde phase, as there's a powerful New Moon solar eclipse in Aries on 29 March. A solar eclipse is a symbol of new beginnings, a turbo-powered New Moon. Use the solar eclipse energy to embrace change and leap into a new adventure. However, ideally wait until mid-April before leaping in. Note that beginnings which coincide with eclipses sometimes come after an ending. One door closes for a new door to open. Either way, life's calling you out to be bold and courageous.

Mercury returns to Aries from 16 April to 10 May, a positive period to get things moving within your career. Think second chances, chase up old contacts and rework your options.

There's another planet retrograde in Aries early in the year – the planet of relating, Venus. Venus turns retrograde on 2 March until 13 April. This coincides with Mercury's retrograde phase, so be aware that this period in the year could be tricky.

Your work relationships could prove challenging and may take up a lot of your energy and time. It's not the best period in the year to sign or seal a deal, even if there's a sense of urgency around starting something new. Your career prospects may be closely tied to other people's decisions. Or you're caught up in a competitive situation and feel pressured into taking on work that isn't yours to do.

Venus returns to Aries from 30 April to 6 June and this coincides with Saturn's move into Aries on 25 May. Get the right people on your side and make the right connections during this period in the year and you could make swift progress. Also, note what happens on 6 April, 5 May and 5 June, as these are dates when the inner planets are moving through Aries and your career and vocation sector and align with lucky Jupiter. Trust your intuition in making a key decision.

There's one more important influence in your career sector and this is Neptune moving into Aries from 30 March to 22 October. Neptune is one of the slower-moving generational planets, so this is a rare occurrence. Neptune will return to Aries next year on 26 January 2026, where it remains until 2038/2039. At its best, Neptune is creative, imaginative and inspirational. You may be full of dreams for your future and what you want to achieve. There's an idealistic quality to Neptune's influence.

In June, July and August, Saturn and Neptune are close together. And, in February 2026, they make an epic conjunction for the first time since 1989. Saturn and Neptune are opposite influences so you may feel torn between different paths. Saturn is materialistic, favouring a conventional or traditional path. Whereas Neptune favours helping others and saving the world. Ideally, try to find the sweet spot where the two planets can work together. Perhaps, you're a mathematician with a side gig in music. Or you're an artist who works in tech. Whatever your personal situation, how can you combine your right brain and your left brain faculties to create something unique?

The period from 15 June to 19 June could be challenging. This is when Jupiter in Cancer clashes with Saturn and Neptune in Aries. Saying yes to a new path in life may seem impossible during this period. If this is true for you, don't equate what happens professionally with who you are as a person. Also, if you hear a calling, don't be scared of trying something different. Notice what occurs in August when Uranus in Gemini teams up with Saturn in Aries on 12 August and Neptune in Aries on 29 August. Be unique or alternative and walk your own path. If you do experience a work crisis or desperately want to change direction in your career but don't know how, try to remain philosophical. Aim to explore all the possibilities and keep your gaze on the future. This isn't necessarily an overnight shift but a long-term project.

Perhaps, you've long held a dream about what you want to do but you've not had the time to commit to your plans. Or you've been putting things off because you felt scared or doubted yourself. Whatever your personal situation, be honest with yourself and visualise what your life would be like if you let yourself fully embrace your dreams.

BIG DREAMER

Dreams are important to you in 2025 because of the major emphasis on your fellow water sign Pisces. The planet linked to dreams and the imagination Neptune has been in Pisces since

2012. This is a creative influence and Pisces is the star sign that pulls you out into the cosmos, the universe. Pisces rules all areas of life that draw you out into the world, whether physically, mentally, intellectually, spiritually or philosophically. It's wherever you find inspiration, meaning and purpose.

But Neptune's dreams don't always become reality unless there's another planetary influence involved. And, since March 2023, Saturn has been in this same sector of your horoscope. This year, Saturn and Neptune are working together and both planets are completing their journey through Pisces. When planets shift star sign, you sense their energy the strongest. This could help you manifest your dreams and turn them into reality.

You may sense a calling early in the year when the North Node enters Pisces on 12 January. This is where it remains until 26 July 2026. The nodes are closely linked to the eclipses, which act as turning points or moments of destiny. Eclipses are significant for you because your ruler is the Moon and eclipses involve the close relationship between the Sun, the Moon and planet Earth.

This year, there are two powerful Full Moon lunar eclipses. The first takes place on 14 March and the second takes place on 7 September. The eclipses cut across the Virgo/Pisces axis of the zodiac, encouraging you to expand your learning, travel somewhere new and embrace life to the full. If you're bored with your everyday life, the eclipses could act as a wake-up call.

Pisces' energy is overflowing during the first few months of the year. This is when the planet of communication, Mercury, and the planet of relating, Venus, are involved. Both planets spend longer than usual in Pisces. Venus is here from 3 January to 4 February, and again from 27 March to 30 April. It's Mercury's turn from 14 February to 3 March, and again from 30 March to 16 April. As both planets move back and forth through Pisces, they connect with the North Node, Saturn and Neptune numerous times. This creates a flow of energy and, somewhere in life, you're going to experience bliss or transcendence. Perhaps, you're an artist, you're on a spiritual path or you like to lose yourself in ecstatic dance or classical concerts. You could sign up for the trip of a lifetime or study a course that's life changing.

This is about your beliefs and principles too. You may have a strong religious faith. Or you feel called to help other people outside of your own community. What takes place this year and what you discover might be the catalyst that leads you down a new path.

There is a proviso here, though, because you can lose yourself in Pisces' realm. Be wary of falling into addictive tendencies and keep coming back to yourself. Find your escape outlet but keep it real.

Your friends may be the ones to inspire you this year and introduce you to new ideas or activities. Uranus is in Taurus and your friendship sector up until 7 July. It's been here since 2018 and this year is significant as it's changing star sign. Uranus in Taurus represents unexpected friendships, which may bring you into contact with an alternative group of people. Perhaps, you're attracted to wild and unconventional characters, the rebels of society. Either way, it's via your friends where you're likely to encounter excitement and inspiration.

Align yourself with the right people in the year ahead and open up your world to infinite possibility.

MONEY MATTERS

This year is likely to be a significant one financially. This is because of a relatively new influence in Aquarius and your joint finance sector. Power planet Pluto has been moving in and out of Aquarius in 2023/2024. This year, Pluto is established in Aquarius for the next twenty years. Pluto is the planet of power and transformation. Therefore, you're wise to dive deep into money matters this year.

On a simple level, this might mean that you're doing online banking in a new way. Aquarius rules technology and systems and Pluto is linked to wealth. You might be transforming your financial investments and you'd be wise to do so. Look to the future and keep one step ahead of the pack.

Get on top of your finances early in the year. The period from 21 January to 3 February is pivotal. Look at ways of making your money work for you and ensure you're getting the best returns on your savings and investments. This may be about improving your money mindset or boosting your sense of value or self-worth. When you value who you are, you can charge for your services accordingly and get paid what you deserve. If you sense that the past is holding you back financially, explore this fully through therapy or self-help books.

Pluto is an extreme planet and it's wise to pay attention wherever Pluto's moving through your horoscope. It's the highs and lows of life. For example, you could experience debt or bankruptcy while Pluto's in your joint finance sector. Alternatively, you could receive an inheritance, a bonus or a major return on investment. Perhaps, you step into your power playing the stock market.

As soon as 2025 begins, you may have a sense that you want

to get on top of your finances and set some new resolutions. However, Leo is your personal money sector and there's been a lot of stop-start activity in Leo since the middle of 2023, so proceed with caution where finances are concerned. More recently, action planet Mars turned retrograde in Leo on 6 December 2024 and Mars remains retrograde until 24 February. On 3 January, Mars is opposite Pluto cutting across the financial axis of your horoscope. This isn't an easy combination. Perhaps you start the year in debt or you have more money going out than coming in. Finances could be topsy-turvy in the first few months of the year with some wins but some losses too. Either way, get ready to push ahead with money matters when Mars returns to Leo from 18 April to 17 June. This is when Mars is in direct motion, strong and assertive, which is great for money-making ventures.

One date to be wary of is 27 April when Mars is once again opposed by Pluto. Notice who you're up against and avoid competitive situations in or around the end of April. What this combination can be good for is being ruthless when it comes to money and making any necessary financial cuts or adjustments.

Later this year, there's another retrograde phase in Leo involving communication planet Mercury. Mercury turns retrograde in Leo from 18 July to 11 August. This is when you're wise to take your foot off the accelerator and not make any major financial decisions or investments. Mercury gives its name to the markets and merchandise, and when Mercury's retrograde, the money markets are often chaotic. Instead, use the Mercury retrograde phase to review and reassess your financial situation. Be a strategist and researcher and put your money-making plans and ideas into action once Mercury turns direct on 11 August.

Pluto's move through Aquarius is urging you to become more

cash savvy. It's important that you get the right experts and financial advisers on your side. Don't stick with someone out of loyalty and put your long-term interests first.

If you're a typical Sun Cancer, you're frugal and a saver rather than a spender. This approach to finances could stand you in good stead in 2025.

LOVE AND CONNECTIONS

The planet of extremes, Pluto, was in Capricorn and your relationship sector from 2008 onwards. It's only in the last two years, 2023/2024, that Pluto has finally departed your opposite star sign. Pluto tends to be an all-or-nothing planet and emotions run deep. You may have been in a relationship with a powerful individual. Or perhaps you fell prey to power and control. Alternatively, you may have met your soul mate and been obsessive about love. Or you called time on a relationship or marriage that wasn't working out.

This is the first year that Pluto is no longer in Capricorn and your relationship sector. You may experience a sense of relief or feel less trapped by your motivations or desire. You may have a stronger sense of your autocracy and find it easier to pursue your personal and higher goals. Or perhaps you're simply no longer bound to someone else and freedom beckons.

Your love stars are most active later this year, especially if you're seeking new romance or a love affair. This is Scorpio's domain and there's plenty happening here from October onwards. There are some gorgeous connections between the inner planets in Scorpio and lucky Jupiter in Cancer. The dates to note are 24 October, 28 October, 17 November, 26 November and 6 December. The only proviso is that Mercury is retrograde from 9 November to 29 November. This can be a time when an ex reappears in your life or you're yearning for a past love. Ideally, wait until the end of November before making up your mind about a love relationship.

Scorpio is a passionate star sign and you have the planet of libido Mars here from 22 September to 4 November, followed by love planet Venus from 6 November to 30 November. Yet, you may only know if a love relationship is true once the inner planets enter Capricorn and your relationship sector. Mars is here from 15 December followed by the Sun on 21 December and love planet Venus on 24 December. This promises a romantic end to 2025 and it could be a peak period for marriage or a long-term relationship.

As a Sun Cancer, your partner planet is Saturn. If you're married or in a long-term relationship, it's wise to look at what Saturn's doing to discover more. As Saturn changes star sign in the middle of the year, your relationship may have to adapt to a new situation. And indeed, you may already have experienced some major changes over the last couple of years that have impacted your home or family life. This is because there's been a powerful eclipse cycle cutting across the Aries/Libra axis of the zodiac and the foundations of your life. Aries rules your career and future path, while Libra rules your home and family, your foundations and roots. This eclipse cycle began in April 2023 and completes in March 2025. It's often a time when you change career, move home or experience major changes within your family.

This year, as Saturn and Neptune move into Aries, they oppose planets in Libra and your home and family sector. The key dates are 9 August, 18 September, 21 September and 14

October. As much as you might want things to remain the same, you may be called to surrender, release or let go, as one chapter comes to an end and a new chapter begins. This may be closely connected to what's happening in your partner's life.

If you're a typical Sun Cancer, your emotional connections are important to you. Yes, you can be a homebody, but being able to express your emotions and have people in your life who you can talk to is paramount. This year, there are not one but two New Moons in Virgo and your communication sector. New Moons promise new beginnings and making new friends.

The first New Moon in Virgo takes place on 23 August, an ideal date to initiate new connections or friendships. The second New Moon is a powerful solar eclipse in Virgo on 21 September, the day before the equinox. Notice who comes into your life on or around this key date as this person could play a vital role in your life moving forward. Or perhaps you're the one who steps in, helping a sibling or neighbour.

You have some lovely planetary aspects connecting Jupiter in your star sign Cancer with key planets in Virgo on 12 September and 8 October, either side of the eclipse. This might coincide with a new social initiative or community event that's collaborative and supportive. Virgo is the star sign of writing and linked to study and schools in your horoscope. You may step into a tutoring or coaching role. Or perhaps you're the one who goes back to school and discovers a new love of learning.

Be open and expansive and bring good people into your life in 2025. Do so and you're likely to create some lasting and loving connections.

RULING PLANET

You're a Moon child as your star sign is ruled by the Moon. Your emotions tend to wax and wane, your moods ebb and flow. The phases of the Moon are important for you so aim to be in tune with the Moon's cycle.

The New Moon is a symbol of new beginnings and a positive period to take the initiative. When you first see the crescent Moon in the night sky, make a wish.

The Full Moon heightens emotions and is a time to trust your intuition and make clear decisions. When the Moon is at its fullest, use this moon phase for magic and ritual. Full Moons represent completion and culmination, a time to release and let go.

All the New and Full Moons in 2025 are in this book (see pages 52–3), so you can write them into your diary.

LUCKY DATES

Full Moon Cancer – achievement/culmination – 13 January

Jupiter enters Cancer – 9 June

Sun conjunct Jupiter Cancer – 24 June

Your New Moon Cancer – new beginnings – 25 June

Venus conjunct Jupiter Cancer – 12 August

Venus Virgo sextile Jupiter Cancer – 8 October

Sun Scorpio trine Jupiter Cancer – 17 November

Venus Scorpio trine Jupiter Cancer – 26 November

LEO

YOUR 2025 HOROSCOPE

LEO RULERSHIPS

ZODIAC SYMBOL: THE LION

RULING PLANET: SUN, LORD OF THE DAY,
BRINGER OF LIGHT AND CONSCIOUSNESS

MODE/ELEMENT: FIXED FIRE –
DETERMINED, ENTHUSIASTIC,
PASSIONATE, COURAGEOUS

COLOUR: GOLD, ORANGE

ARCHETYPE: THE PERFORMER,
KING/QUEEN OF THE JUNGLE

YOUR TOP TIPS FOR 2025

LEAD A NEW GROUP, REVOLUTIONISE
YOUR FRIENDSHIPS

WORK WITH VULNERABLE PEOPLE,
PRIORITISE SELF-CARE

TAKE A WORK SABBATICAL,
EXPLORE LIVING ABROAD

BECOME A FINANCIAL WIZARD

CREATE RELATIONSHIPS BASED
ON EQUALITY

Ω

FRIENDS AND GROUPS

Jupiter is the biggest planet in the universe and the best planet in astrology. It's always helpful to notice in which sector of your horoscope Jupiter is active, as this is where new opportunities, growth and expansion lie. As 2025 begins, Jupiter is in air sign Gemini, where it's been since 25 May 2024. Jupiter will remain there until 9 June.

Gemini rules friends, groups and social activities in your horoscope, your alliances and associations. This is an ideal time to find people of like minds and make sure that your social life is not only fun but interesting and enlightening. While Jupiter's in Gemini, bring new friends into your life and make an effort to catch up with old friends. Jupiter may create the opportunities, perhaps through a friend's wedding, anniversary or school reunion. All you have to do is say yes.

This would also be a good time to take what you do out into the wider world and get people on board who can help you. This is about gathering people around you – a team that can work alongside you and make your life easier and more enjoyable. Being a Sun Leo, you like to take centre stage somewhere in your life and you make a great organiser or boss. In the universe, all the planets orbit around your ruler, the Sun, and they are essential to one another. Use this as a symbol in your own life. While Jupiter's in Gemini, if you've been trying to do too much alone, your stars are urging you to reach out and reconnect.

See who comes into your life on or around 30 January and 3 February. This is when key planets in Aquarius and your partnership sector connect with Jupiter in Gemini. Make the right moves and you could gain influential support that benefits you. Also, notice what happens on 6 April, 5 May and 5 June, when the inner planets moving through Aries and your travel and study sector align with Jupiter. These would be promising dates to travel or go on holiday, take a test or exam. Or perhaps you could attend a workshop or conference which expands your knowledge and learning.

The stand-out date is 8 June when there's a Mercury–Jupiter conjunction in Gemini. You might be proud of a friend on or around this date. Or perhaps you're the one who's celebrating and you're gathering your friends around you. Make the most of this social and educational combination and line up something special.

Notice who you meet on or around these key dates and what opportunities arise, as anything that begins under Jupiter's gaze promises success.

Take this powerful symbolism out into the world too. Whether you're into politics, humanitarian or environmental causes, social change or social reform, it's an ideal time to join in and play your part.

Gemini is the sign of communication and the emphasis on air signs this year is about the information networks. Notice the connections between you and others, both visible and invisible. Reach out, share ideas and find your tribe.

The emphasis on your friendship and group sector doesn't

end when Jupiter leaves Gemini. In fact, Jupiter's move through one of the social sectors of your horoscope could start something in your life that becomes an unstoppable force. This is because another major planet moves into this sector of your horoscope on 7 July – innovative Uranus, the planet of change. Uranus takes approximately seven years to move through one star sign, so this is a major shift. Uranus stays in Gemini until 8 November but will return next year on 26 April 2026. Then, Uranus will remain in your friendship sector until 2032/2033.

Uranus's energy is innovative, experimental and alternative. Therefore, be open-minded and curious about your friendships and group connections. Yet, Uranus can be about splits and cutting off too. You may recognise that you've outgrown certain people in your life. Or that you're ready to leave behind a social or online group that's played a significant role in your personal development.

Uranus rules all things new, including technology, the new age and futuristic ideas. You may choose to explore an alternative group when Uranus is in Gemini. Or you team up with people who have an unusual hobby or a different perspective on life. Perhaps, you become interested in space travel, learn electronics or start a radical new group or revolution. Notice what happens when Uranus is active on 12 August and 29 August. What you get involved in could open up a new future path in your life, linked to education, religion or new ideologies.

One thing's for sure, when Uranus is in your friendship and group sector, this is where you're advised to press the refresh button. Take a fresh look at your current set of friends and group connections. This includes political alliances, community groups and society in general. Where do you fit in and how do you want to make your mark or make a difference? Are you being called to be a rebel or radical or are you discovering a new way of seeing the world?

Your astrology indicates that 2025 is a year when you're going to be considering your role within relationships and with others in general. This is where there's prominent focus in your horoscope in the year ahead.

CARING AND CONNECTING

Jupiter changes star sign on 9 June and moves into Cancer, where it will remain until 30 June 2026. Jupiter in Cancer turns your attention towards the most hidden sector of your horoscope, the star sign before yours. This is an opportunity to focus on your inner world, develop your spirituality or learn to put your trust and faith in life and the universe. This could indicate a period in which you choose to explore life beyond the everyday and push back the boundaries of what's possible.

Get to know yourself and the universe on a deeper or more expansive level. Jupiter is a protective influence and water sign Cancer is kind and caring. Therefore, this combination is encouraging you to love yourself and others. Prioritise self-care or step into a role as carer or guardian.

Sometimes, when Jupiter's in Cancer, you're wise to take your foot off the accelerator of life, to choose silence or go on retreat. Do whatever works for you so you can listen to your inner voice. Or perhaps you're working on something behind the scenes, doing research or planning ahead for a new phase in your life. Think of this as a key time of preparation. This is paving the way for Jupiter's move into your star sign next year. It takes Jupiter twelve years to circuit the zodiac and you'll benefit from Jupiter's bounty and good fortune in 2026/2027.

In astrology, working with timing is the key to your success. Early in the year, action planet Mars is retrograde in Cancer from 6 January to 24 February. This isn't a time when you can get ahead. Mars retrograde often signifies a stop-start scenario. Perhaps you experience a bout of illness or your energy levels are low. Consider what's stopping you from pursuing your personal goals. Don't push too hard at the start of the year and avoid taking a wrong turn or running in the wrong direction.

Mars in Cancer can be an anxious placing for you, when your mind kicks into overdrive. You might lack the confidence you need to be out in the world. Or perhaps you want to hibernate or retreat more. Mars is the planet of anger, so be wary of being self-critical and putting yourself down. This is a time when you're wise to be extra caring of your precious self and kind to your inner child. Prioritise self-care during the start of the year or start on a healing journey. There's no rush as 2025 begins.

Your ruler, the Sun, joins Jupiter in Cancer on 21 June, the day of the solstice. One of the luckiest conjunctions of the year takes place during this period, when the Sun and Jupiter come together in Cancer on 24 June. This could coincide with a spiritual revelation or awakening as the Sun illuminates and Jupiter expands. Alternatively, you receive good news from a private benefactor or experience good fortune because of your connections to the past. The cycle of karma is closely connected to planets in the hidden sector of your horoscope. This can be a time when past favours are repaid.

Another powerful conjunction in Cancer takes place on 12 August when the planet of love and money Venus sits next to

Jupiter, the two best planets coming together. You might choose to invest in a charity or worthy cause and put your caring credentials to good use. Alternatively, you may attend a ritual or sign up for a course that teaches you about the law of attraction.

Perhaps you're on a trip down memory lane in the middle of the year. It would be a wonderful time to go on holiday with family, to honour and appreciate your past connections.

There may be a lucrative influence too, as Jupiter is linked to wealth and abundance. Perhaps you're fundraising for a retreat or refuge. Or you're sharing resources with family to secure your future prospects.

As the inner planets move through Virgo and your personal money sector, they team up with Jupiter in Cancer on 22 June, 12 September and 8 October. These are positive dates for investments or asking for money, if you're the one in need.

Then, Jupiter in Cancer aligns with planets in Scorpio and your home and family sector in the last few months of the year. The key dates are 24 October, 28 October, 17 November, 26 November and 6 December. This emphasises the importance of investing in these key areas of your life. You might be dealing with an inheritance or preserving memories from the past. Perhaps you return to live somewhere you grew up or you spent time previously. This may be about protecting your own family, your wider family or other people who come under your care. This could also be the world family – e.g. opening your home to refugees or caring for those in society who are vulnerable.

Whatever you're involved in during the last few months of the year, be aware that Mercury is retrograde from 9 November to 29 November. This is a time to review your situation, rather than make a big decision or major investment. Ideally, wait until

Mercury turns direct in Scorpio and your home and family sector on 29 November before finalising an agreement or signing and sealing a deal. This could include a property deal.

When Jupiter's in Cancer, this is encouraging you to move away from the ego, to surrender to life and find your own form of prayer or spirituality. This may be closely linked to your generous heart and your natural-born ability to help other people. Jupiter in Cancer is self-less rather than self-centred.

Most important during Jupiter's journey through Cancer is to take care of yourself, before you reach out to help others. Ensure there's a deep well of inner strength and replenish the wellness pot whenever it runs dry.

STUDY AND DEVOTION

During 2025, there are some major planetary shifts including the planet of authority and responsibility, Saturn, changing star sign. This only happens once every two to three years. On 25 May, Saturn enters your fellow fire sign Aries where it remains until 1 September. Saturn will return to Aries next year from 14 February 2026 to April 2028. Aries rules travel and study in your horoscope, and where you find meaning and purpose. It's whatever takes you beyond the mundane side of life and urges you to explore and learn. Saturn's move through Aries may reconnect you with a spiritual or religious path or a desire for knowledge.

You may be ready to commit to a period of study, perhaps a two- to three-year course. Or you might be considering a major move abroad or relocating to a different area of the country. Saturn's move through Aries is encouraging you to focus on your long-term goals and where it may benefit you to gain qualifications or accreditation. You could become a teacher or a student, whatever's right for you. It's an ideal time to consider where you're heading and why.

Alternatively, there could be a realisation that one dream may not happen, once Saturn enters Aries. This is because Saturn rules endings as well as hard work and commitment. Review and reassess when Saturn changes star sign.

The focus on travel and study has been calling you for a while. This is because of the Aries/Libra eclipse cycle which began in April 2023 and completes in March 2025. Eclipses represent the turning points of life when you're being called in a new direction. In 2023 and 2024, there have already been two New Moon solar eclipses in Aries. And, on 29 March, the third and final solar eclipse takes place in your travel and study sector. What are you saying yes to on or around this powerful turning point? Solar eclipses are turbo-powered New Moons, urging you to be proactive and bold.

This period in the year coincides with two planets turning retrograde in Aries, so timing is the key to your success. Talk planet Mercury is retrograde from 15 March to 7 April, and the planet of relating, Venus, is on go slow from 2 March to 13 April. Therefore, consider this period in the year as a time of exploration. It may benefit you to go away, to be somewhere different that gives you a fresh perspective on your life. When planets are retrograde, the important changes take place on the inside. Perhaps, you take time out early in the year to immerse yourself in a study project or revision.

You might return somewhere you've visited before. This might be somewhere you have a karmic connection with and feel inexplicably drawn towards its culture and what it represents to you. Retrograde phases are ideal for reconnecting with people and places from the past.

A notable date may be 23 March, when your ruler, the Sun, teams up with Venus retrograde in Aries. This combination conjures up the theme of the divine feminine. Perhaps, you're developing a training course for women or people from different cultures. You may come together with other women to further a longing for reunion or communion with the divine. This may be the start of your own inner awakening when you start to develop and pursue a religious or spiritual path.

Another key planet moves into Aries this year – Neptune, god of the sea. Neptune will be in your travel and study sector from 30 March to 22 October. Neptune is one of the slower-moving generational planets. Neptune will return to Aries on 26 January 2026, where it will remain until 2038/2039. Neptune has a devotional nature, as it's the planet of ecstasy and bliss. Neptune in Aries will contribute to this calling to move beyond the everyday and seek higher meaning and purpose in your life.

Saturn and Neptune are close together in Aries throughout June, July and August. They will meet in February 2026, for the first time since 1989. Together in Aries, these two planets represent the teacher, the shaman, the spiritual leader. Perhaps you're the one stepping into this role. Or you're on a mission to find your teacher, guru or guide. You're being called to walk the path of wisdom, knowledge and higher learning. This is about idealism too and standing up for what you believe in. You might step into a political role, become more involved in cross-cultural groups or volunteer for a charity that's based abroad.

Saturn and Neptune in Aries won't necessarily stop you

feeling fearful about what comes next. In fact, it may be your fears for the future which drive you to take action and make strong commitments in your life. This may be a case of 'feel the fear and do it anyway'.

Be disciplined in your endeavours and develop a habit of daily study or prayer. Saturn and Neptune need to work together to be effective in your life. This means keeping your explorations grounded in reality, which will help you avoid falling for a cult or being seduced or swayed by dogma.

JUGGLING FINANCES

The planet of responsibility, Saturn, is starting to complete its journey through Pisces and your joint finance sector in 2025. This is where Saturn's been since March 2023. Pisces is the star sign linked to all financial transactions, including inheritance, investments, savings, debt, taxes and loans. Sometimes, when Saturn's in this sector of your horoscope, money's scarce. Or you have to work harder than usual to keep your money safe and secure. Saturn is rarely a light influence, although it can lend you discipline and self-mastery.

Saturn moves out of your finance sector on 25 May, although it returns here from 1 September through to 14 February 2026. Therefore, it's wise to ask what's coming to an end financially. This may require something new from you, perhaps a shift in attitude or a new money mindset.

It's also notable that Neptune is starting to leave Pisces this year, having been there since 2012. On the plus side, Neptune in Pisces favours dreams and the imagination to conjure up money-making ideas. On the minus side, money can slip through your fingers as Neptune's the planet linked to seduction and betrayal. Neptune will leave Pisces on 30 March and return for one final time from 22 October to 26 January 2026.

Pisces' energy kicks in big time during the first few months of the year. This is because of an overload of activity in Pisces, thanks to two planets spending an unusually long time in your joint finance sector. Talk planet Mercury is in Pisces from 14 February to 3 March, and again from 30 March to 16 April. Also, the planet of relating, Venus, is in Pisces from 3 January to 4 February, and again from 27 March to 30 April. And both planets will spend time retrograde during March and April. Therefore, it seems likely that finances will be a major influence in your life in the first four months of the year. You might be involved in a business merger or a personal project that's a long-term investment. Perhaps you have a lot of financial responsibilities or some significant change impacts your fortunes. It's a heady mix of activity that may leave you feeling overwhelmed or confused about what's next. Try not to let your heart lead your head. Ideally, balance both when negotiating finances. And, most importantly, put off making any major financial decisions until mid-April when both Mercury and Venus complete their retrograde phases.

There's another factor involved which involves the eclipses and the nodes. The nodes are linked to the path of destiny and, on 12 January, the North Node enters Pisces, where it will remain until 26 July 2026. This adds a fateful feel to finances as the wheel of fortune turns. You could do extremely well under this planetary influence if you play your cards right.

Notice what happens when the eclipses kick in, as they cut across the Virgo/Pisces axis of the zodiac and the financial axis of your horoscope. This year, there are two Full Moon lunar eclipses on 14 March and 7 September. Eclipses in your finance sector can be a time of swings and roundabouts. For example, you win big on the lottery but end up paying out a lot on tax.

Keep your cards close to your chest during eclipse season. This isn't the time to give too much away unless you can afford it and you're on a mission to get rid of your money and all your possessions. Though that would be an extreme example. More likely is that you invest in a project that can help others and the charitable side of your nature kicks in.

Get on the right side of other people – perhaps an influencer, sponsor or legal eagle. If you're in the midst of a fundraising campaign, you could do unusually well with so much emphasis on your money sectors.

Also this year, there are not one but two New Moons in Virgo and your personal money sector. New Moons are a symbol of new beginnings, an ideal time to set your intentions or, in this situation, launch a money-making project. The first New Moon takes place on 23 August and the second on 21 September, the day before the equinox, plus it's a solar eclipse. This is a New Moon with turbo power and the seeds that you sow during this eclipse could flourish and bear fruit in the future.

Admittedly, you need to be bold when it comes to finances. At the same time, you're wise to tread carefully with so much activity in these key areas of your horoscope. Yet, juggle your finances well during 2025 and you could win big.

CAREER AND VOCATION

The planet Uranus has been in Taurus and your career and future sector since 2018. This year, Uranus remains in Taurus until 7 July and returns to Taurus from 8 November to 26 April 2026. Otherwise, Uranus is on the move.

Uranus is the planet of change linked to freedom, also splits and separation. It favours the new over the old, the unconventional and unique over the traditional. It's been a huge motivator in your career and vocational sector in recent years and you may be more acutely aware of Uranus's influence as it prepares to move on. Uranus is especially active during Taurus season, from 19 April to 20 May, when your ruler, the Sun, is in Taurus. There's a New Moon here on 27 April, a symbol of new beginnings. You could land a new job or hear of a new opportunity that's right up your street.

Also, there are some exciting planetary conjunctions involving Uranus on 17 May, 24 May and, later in the year, on 4 July. These dates are when you may be ready to go freelance, jump ship or take a leap of faith. Uranus favours impulsive action and the lure of the new. It's the planet linked to technology and all things futuristic and modern. You may already be on a new path in life. Or your values are changing and you're more interested in freedom than status and reputation.

You're wise to make any significant move linked to your career or vocation earlier in the year rather than later. The stars incline, they do not compel, and you're going to lose innovative Uranus from your career sector in 2026. Plus, if you wait to move things forward until later in 2025, your situation could change again. This is because Uranus is unusually busy in a run of planetary oppositions. The key dates are 19 November, 21 November, 30 November and 10 December. This coincides with Mercury retrograde from 9 November to 29 November. This is when you may find that the work/life balance is out of kilter and life steps in to change things around. Or perhaps what's happening at home or within your family takes priority and you have to change your path accordingly. Uranus is the planet of the unexpected and events in November could mean you have to shift direction and fast.

Money and career are inextricably linked in your life in 2025. Events on or around 4 April and 20 November could reveal why. You might see what's possible, also what's not possible.

Uranus comes along to wake you up, to encourage you to embrace change and move into the future. Make the most of the planet of innovation, invention and revolution stirring up your career and future sector one last time, before it continues its journey to a different sector of your horoscope.

LOVE AND PARTNERSHIP

Throughout 2023/2024, power planet Pluto has been moving in and out of Aquarius and your relationship sector. This year, Pluto is established in Aquarius, where it will remain for the next twenty years. You may attract a powerful partner into your life with Pluto in Aquarius, either personally or professionally. Alternatively, you might find the willpower to ditch a dead-end relationship or a business partnership that smacks of power and control.

Certainly, it's not a year to take love for granted or stay put doing the same thing. Pluto's the planet of transformation, urging you to go in deep when it comes to love. Perhaps, you enter into therapy as a couple or you embark on a course of personal development. At its best, Pluto power is about finding a soul-mate connection and discovering intimacy on a whole new level. However, it's also worth knowing that Pluto was god of the underworld in mythology and has a link to corruption and underhand business. Therefore, be careful not to get involved with the wrong kind of person. Aquarius rules enemies in your life and you don't want to get on the wrong side of someone who can bring trouble. Be savvy when it comes to your one-to-ones.

There may be times this year when you find yourself up against strong opposition. This is because of what's happening with planets in Leo and your personal sector. As the year begins, action planet Mars is moving backwards through your star sign Leo and immediately encounters Pluto on 3 January. This may mean you are in a weakened position as the year begins. Or perhaps you're determined to take a step back from a competitive relationship or a situation that's potentially dangerous. You refuse to get involved. As Mars is retrograde until 24 February, you're wise to slow things down and rework your strategy. Get ready to do battle once again when Mars is strong in Leo from 18 April to 17 June.

Even though Mars gives you energy and courage, Pluto's powerful in opposition on 27 April and again on 29 June, 25 July and 27 August. These are all dates to be wary of around partnerships, both personal and professional. You may find you're under attack. Perhaps you're involved in court proceedings or you're up against someone whose behaviour is cruel or punishing. Stand your ground if necessary and find your inner strength.

Since the middle of 2023, you've been on a journey of personal discovery. This is because all the inner planets, Venus, Mars and Mercury, have been retrograde in your star sign Leo. This is often a time of personal insight and learning on a deep level. In the middle of this year, talk planet Mercury turns retrograde in Leo from 18 July to 11 August. This is another chance to get to know yourself better. True happiness stems from loving yourself first. Keep your options open while Mercury's retrograde in November but go all out to get what you want in December.

If you're looking for love in 2025, there's major activity in Sagittarius, your romance sector, later in the year. Passion planet Mars is here from 4 November to 15 December and the planet of love, Venus, is in Sagittarius from 30 November to 24 December. This is a peak period for meeting someone new or enlivening your sex life, if you're currently in a relationship or married. Sagittarius rules children and pregnancy in your horoscope and it's an especially fertile period if you're looking to start a family.

Your ruler, the Sun, joins the Sagittarius party from 22 November to 21 December, and Mercury extends the feel-good vibes over the festive period. 2025 may be a year when you're getting used to Pluto in your relationship sector, but don't let that stop you embracing passion while the planets are on your side.

RULING PLANET

As a Leo, you are ruled by the Sun; the Sun is the centre of the universe and all the other planets revolve around it. Therefore, somewhere in your life, you too can take centre stage as other people move around you. This may be in your community, your family or out in the wider world.

The Sun's job is to shine bright, share warmth, vitality and energy. If you're a typical Leo, you're at your best when you feel these qualities in your life. Be a Sun-seeker and be open to receive acknowledgement, compliments and recognition for the person you are.

The journey of the Sun through the zodiac is your constant, your guiding star. As a Leo, track the progress of the Sun through the star signs and find your natural rhythm within the Sun's rising and setting. Be in tune with the Sun and you are guaranteed more beauty and constancy in your life.

Here are the dates when the Sun is in each of the twelve star signs, revealing which area of your life is under the cosmic spotlight. This is where you can shine most brightly.

Until 19 January: Capricorn – work and health

19 January to 18 February: Aquarius – relationships and contracts

18 February to 20 March: Pisces – shared finances and esoteric subjects

20 March to 19 April: Aries – travel, study and new horizons

19 April to 20 May: Taurus – career and vocation

20 May to 21 June: Gemini – friends and wider society

21 June to 22 July: Cancer – retreat and inner work

22 July to 22 August: Leo – personal goals and self-image

22 August to 22 September: Virgo – money and values

22 September to 23 October: Libra – local community and communication

23 October to 22 November: Scorpio – home and family

22 November to 21 December: Sagittarius – what you give birth to i.e. children, romance, creative projects

21 December onwards: Capricorn – work and health

LUCKY DATES

Sun Aquarius trine Jupiter Gemini – 30 January

Your Full Moon Leo – achievement/culmination – 12 February

Sun Aries sextile Jupiter Gemini – 6 April

Sun conjunct Jupiter Cancer – 24 June

Your New Moon Leo – new beginnings – 24 July

Mercury turns direct in Leo – 11 August

Sun Virgo sextile Jupiter Cancer – 12 September

Sun Scorpio trine Jupiter Cancer – 17 November

VIRGO

YOUR 2025 HOROSCOPE

VIRGO RULERSHIPS

ZODIAC SYMBOL: THE VIRGIN

RULING PLANET: MERCURY,
THE COMMUNICATOR AND WRITER

MODE/ELEMENT: MUTABLE EARTH –
CLEVER, AGILE, CRAFTY, HANDS ON

COLOUR: NATURAL, EARTHY COLOURS

ARCHETYPE: THE CRITIC,
THE QUEEN (OR KING) OF CLEAN

YOUR TOP TIPS FOR 2025

GO FOR PROMOTION, BE A VOICE
OF THE PEOPLE

START A NEW GROUP, GET CLOSER
TO FRIENDS WHO LIVE ABROAD

INVEST IN ETHICAL BANKING,
SPEND LESS/SAVE MORE

DIVE DEEP INTO LOVE,
COMMIT TO A RELATIONSHIP

TRANSFORM YOUR BODY,
PRIORITISE YOUR HEALTH

♍

CAREER AND VOCATION

Jupiter is the planet of luck and opportunity, the biggest and best planet. As 2025 begins, Jupiter is moving through Gemini and the star sign at the peak of your horoscope. Gemini represents your career and vocation, your status and reputation. It's about your future path and your public profile. Jupiter entered Gemini on 25 May 2024 where it remains until 9 June. This has to be a healthy boost to your ambitions. Jupiter in Gemini offers you a chance to play big, fly high and expand your horizons. The biggest planet represents opportunity, growth and expansion. And, in your career and vocation sector, Jupiter is a symbol of the free spirit and entrepreneur.

Your star sign is ruled by Mercury, the planet of communication. Gemini is the other star sign ruled by fleet-footed Mercury. In mythology, Mercury was the messenger of the gods and there's a nimble, quick nature to Mercury. Bear this in mind as Jupiter in Gemini, Mercury's star sign, may be about multitasking or adding another string to your bow.

Gemini and Virgo rule the spoken and written word. So this might be a positive time for you to pursue a career linked to communication or sharing your message with the world. You could become head librarian or set up a niche publishing company. You might start an online shop or get involved with a community initiative trading skills.

Plus, Jupiter connects you with the world, as it's the global planet. This is an ideal time to reach out to other people to expand your career. Make the most of your networks and connections. Plan work abroad or take a sabbatical to study something you've always dreamed of. Leave behind the nine-to-five, go freelance or set up your own business. It's your choice but the opportunity is there, whatever your personal vision.

At its best, Jupiter brings new opportunities, success and a wealth of work. You may find a way to break free from the daily grind and follow your true vocation. Or perhaps you're thinking 'now or never' regarding a specific career ambition. Jupiter in Gemini teams up with planets in Aquarius and your work sector on 30 January and 3 February. If you're on the verge of seeking promotion or looking for a new job, make the most of this. Aquarius rules technology, so use the internet to expand your reach.

Money and career come together on 6 April, 5 May and 5 June. This is when Jupiter in Gemini teams up with the inner planets in Aries and your joint finance sector. Ask for a raise, apply for a loan or set up a joint venture. You have luck and good fortune on your side when Jupiter's in action. The best period in the year for career goals and future developments is arguably Gemini season. The Sun enters Gemini on 20 May and a few days later, on 26 May, your ruling planet, Mercury, moves into Gemini where it remains until 8 June. Importantly, this is the date of a powerful Mercury–Jupiter conjunction in Gemini, your career and vocation sector. Whatever you're working towards in the first few months of the year, this is when you could be successful.

Mercury and Jupiter working together are great for anything to do with universities, higher education, publishing, travel and the law. This might be the year you add letters to your name. Or perhaps you win a writing or journalism award. Go all out to achieve your career and vocation goals while you have Jupiter on your side.

Jupiter's leading the way through Gemini but there's another significant planet moving into Gemini in 2025. That planet is innovative Uranus, which enters Gemini and the star sign of communication for the first time in over eighty years. Uranus moves into Gemini on 7 July where it remains until 8 November. Uranus will return to Gemini next year on 26 April 2026 and stays here until 2032/2033.

The first time a planet enters a new star sign, take note of what happens. Uranus is the planet of change, linked to the unexpected. You could receive an email, text or other communication that turns your life around.

This would be an excellent time to launch a website or experiment with a new and different activity. Uranus is the planet of spontaneity and originality, and is linked to technology, new-age thinking and all things modern.

You may lean more towards freelance work with Uranus in your career sector. Or perhaps you're ready for a clean break from your current career and are keen to start something new. Uranus's influence encourages you to seize the day and is a reminder that life's short. It's a radical and revolutionary influence at the peak of your horoscope. You could be ready to disrupt the status quo. Or you choose to update your current place of work and bring it into the present day. Uranus favours all things modern and futuristic. Perhaps, you develop an app or take a radical approach to your business systems or strategies.

You could discover your inner innovator or inventor and you may have more ideas than you can implement. You could shock others with your words or start a ground-breaking podcast. It's your shout but use this electric, fast-paced planetary energy to create waves and leap into the future.

The best month to invest in a new business or new ideas would be August. Stand-out dates linking career innovations and money matters are 12 August and 29 August. You might apply for a loan or start a fundraising campaign online.

Uranus represents the society you live in and Uranus in Gemini is about improving your community or your neighbourhood. Perhaps, you start a petition for better public transport or lead a community group to save your local library or community centre. Use Uranus in Gemini to your benefit and be a voice of the people.

FEEL-GOOD FRIENDSHIPS

Big planet Jupiter changes star sign on 9 June, when it enters water sign Cancer and a slower influence kicks in. Jupiter in Gemini is fast and furious; things tend to happen quickly. You might have too much going on or be juggling too many different career or volunteering options. While Jupiter in Cancer is a reminder not to go it alone but to create a strong network of people around you. This is because Cancer rules the sector of your horoscope that highlights friends, groups, social activities and your wider network.

Jupiter will remain in Cancer until 30 June 2026. This is about finding people you enjoy spending time with and making sure that your social life is not only fun but supportive too.

Bring friends together through activities close to home and make an effort to catch up with old friends. Jupiter in Cancer may create the opportunities for this, perhaps through a friend's wedding, anniversary or school reunion. Two of the best dates for social get-togethers are 24 June and 12 August, when there are gorgeous conjunctions between the Sun and Venus in Cancer with expansive Jupiter. Gather the clans and reach out to your wider family. Throw a party or invite people round to your place to share food and company.

Jupiter in Cancer is a protective influence and can bring out the caring and protective side of your Virgo nature. There's power in connections. Dig deep to learn more about your friends and create strong ties that can't be broken. Whether you're transforming other people's lives or your own life is being shaped and developed through your connections with others, this is where emotional fulfilment lies.

Also, Jupiter rules freedom. Therefore, this could offer you an opportunity to move away from a group situation that's no longer working out. While Jupiter's in Cancer, spread your wings, go global and seek a wider family of people who can help you feel more connected to life and humanity. You could start a chess club or enjoy playing bridge, bowls or badminton in your local neighbourhood. It doesn't matter whether you join the local golf club or step into a leading role with Amnesty International. What matters is that you recognise the power of connections and widen your social circle and your circle of influence. Don't get too caught up with technology and limit your time on social media.

All the inner planets are moving through Virgo this year and, as they do so, they connect with Jupiter in Cancer. The key dates are 22 June, 12 September and 8 October. Jupiter's move through Cancer is a reminder that people count and human connections are vital for your own emotional well-being and the future of our planet, so don't forget to reach out. Jupiter in Cancer favours hugs and counselling, being there for your best friends and reminding other people that they're not alone. This can help you feel less alone and more connected too.

There are more feel-good community vibes when the inner planets move through Scorpio and your communication sector. The key dates are 24 October, 28 October, 17 November, 26 November and 6 December. The flow of good fortune is moving between your community and your wider social network. You could find the right person to help you. Or you have some deep and connecting conversations that benefit everyone.

These combinations favour education, whether you're the teacher or the student. Learn a new skill or attend a group where people can share their opinions and thoughts. You could encourage a friend to take up counselling or find solace through communication.

Scorpio is the star sign which rules siblings, close relatives and neighbours in your horoscope. It's an ideal time to deepen your connections with others.

Be aware that your planet, Mercury, turns retrograde during this period and is on go slow from 9 November to 29 November. Mercury turns retrograde in Sagittarius – your home and family sector – and turns direct in Scorpio – your community and communication sector. This can be a time of misunderstandings and it may be harder to get to the truth of a situation. Take a step back if there's a falling out or misunderstanding. Wait for Mercury to switch direction to reach out and reopen the lines of communication.

Money is one area of life where you're wise to be cautious

when it comes to friends and groups in your life, especially between 15 June and 19 June. When it comes to helping others, do so emotionally but keep your money in your pocket. This isn't an ideal time to loan money to a friend or invest in a group, club or society. You're wise to keep your finances and your friendships separate.

FINANCIAL COMMITMENTS

Finances are under the cosmic spotlight in 2025 and there are a few reasons why. Most importantly, the planet of responsibility, Saturn, shifts gear and moves into Aries, the star sign which rules joint finances and shared resources in your horoscope. Saturn is one of the slower-moving planets and spends approximately two-to-three years in each star sign. Saturn enters Aries on 25 May where it remains until 1 September. Saturn moves into Aries again on 14 February 2026 until April 2028.

In your horoscope, Aries rules all joint money arrangements, such as inheritance, investment, savings and debts, taxes, mortgages, pensions, child maintenance and alimony, loans and joint ventures. As Saturn will remain in this sector of your horoscope for a couple of years, view this as a wake-up call to create some structure to your financial affairs. Get your accounts in order and play a long-term game financially, as this will help you feel more secure. It's a good time to get serious about money and investment and what it means to you. What takes place when Saturn is in Aries could set a precedent for your finances or be the official start of a new financial phase.

Saturn is the planet of endings, as well as commitment, discipline and long-term goals. Saturn's not always a cheery influence in your finance sector, as it represents hard work, persistence and sensible strategies. Saturn prefers to save not spend. Therefore, there's strong planetary energy for planning for the future and cutting out any expenses that are no longer necessary.

At least Saturn has a reputation of getting the job done. Things may have been rocky recently on the financial front. This is because of the eclipse cycle that's been cutting across the Aries/Libra axis of the zodiac. This started in April 2023 and it completes in March 2025. Eclipses represent the highs and low of life, when the wheel of fortune turns and life speeds up. When the eclipses fall in your finance sectors, it can be a time of wins or losses. What rarely happens is that finances are steady and stable.

There's a final eclipse in this cycle on 29 March, a New Moon solar eclipse in Aries. New Moons are about new beginnings but a solar eclipse sometimes indicates a beginning that emerges from an ending.

Notice what's calling you on or around the eclipse. You may be keen to take advantage of a new financial deal. However, you're wise to wait until mid-April before making any major decision or investment. This is because there are two planets retrograde during this period in the year. Venus turns retrograde on 2 March and your ruling planet, Mercury turns retrograde on 15 March. Both planets are linked to money in astrology and this double whammy of retrograde phases means you're wise to play a waiting game, rather than leap in.

Mercury turns direct on 7 April and Venus turns direct on 13 April. This is when new information may come to light that helps you make a clear financial decision. Mercury is back in Aries from 16 April to 10 May and Venus moves back through Aries from 30 April to 6 June, when both planets are moving in the right direction. This means there might be a lot to sort out and negotiate when it comes to finances, personally or professionally. Aim to work alongside other people and get the right experts on your side. Your finances may go further when you're in partnership.

There is another important influence in Aries this year. On 30 March, the planet Neptune moves into Aries where it remains until 22 October. Like Saturn, Neptune will be back in Aries next year on 26 January 2026, where it stays for the following twelve years. Saturn and Neptune are close together in the zodiac in June, July and August. They are preparing to make an epic conjunction in Aries in February 2026. This doesn't happen often – the last time was 1989. Saturn is linked to the material world while Neptune is linked to the spiritual world. Theoretically they are a conflict of interests. How will this play out in your joint finance sector?

It could mean that your values around money are changing. If status and reputation are important to you, perhaps you become more idealistic and recognise the limitations of money. You may feel less secure with these two planets highlighting your financial future. There may be guilt, fear or doubt around money and investments. If you're struggling financially, it's important to tap into your earth sign common sense and face the reality of your situation. Also, be wary of being seduced or scammed.

It may be more important to you where your money goes – i.e. you become a strong advocate of ethical banking and using your money for worthy causes. Think about what you do with your money and examine your financial associations and part-nerships more closely. It's likely that your social conscience will play a significant part in your future success.

LOVE AND RELATIONSHIPS

It could be a significant year for you when it comes to love and relationships. Firstly, your relationships are under the cosmic spotlight because of the current eclipse cycle cutting across the Virgo/Pisces axis of the zodiac. These are the most personal sectors of your horoscope. This eclipse cycle began in September 2024 and will complete in February 2027.

Eclipses often coincide with dramatic events and they accelerate growth. It's hard to stay stuck in your comfort zone when you have eclipse energy propelling you forward. This year, there are two Full Moon lunar eclipses: one in Virgo on 14 March and one in Pisces on 7 September. The wheel of fortune is turning and the eclipses could coincide with an exciting time for love and partnership.

However, it's worth noting that you may have to let go of control. You're not necessarily going to be the one calling the shots. Also, falling in love deeply is often an immersive experience that means you're not in control.

What's important with eclipses is that they can change your situation around. Therefore, if you're in a relationship or married, you may have to confront a personal issue or challenge that develops. Alternatively, if you're single, you could meet someone unexpectedly and your life turns upside down. Either way, it's important to be aware of the eclipse dates and prepare for them. Don't take your close relationships for granted.

Another significant planetary shift influencing relationships involves Saturn changing star sign. Since March 2023, Saturn has been in Pisces and your relationship sector. This year, Saturn will leave Pisces on 25 May and return to Pisces for one last time from 1 September to 14 February 2026.

Wherever Saturn goes, you have to work a little harder. Perhaps a relationship or marriage has been tough going over the last two years with Saturn in your relationship sector. You may have left a relationship or you spent more time on your own. Saturn represents commitment too. It's rarely a light and fluffy influence.

Saturn changing star sign suggests that things are shifting and changing on the relationship front. It may be that the serious work is done and dusted in a relationship, and, you're ready to embrace more fun and lightness as you move forward together. Alternatively, you may be recognising the challenges within a partnership and you know it's time to put some new relationship boundaries in place.

The other planet that's starting its journey away from Pisces is Neptune, Pisces' co-ruler. Neptune is the planet of fantasy, dreams and the imagination. It's linked to glamour and the Hollywood movies, fairytales and romance. Neptune entered Pisces in 2012. This year, Neptune leaves Pisces on 30 March and returns to Pisces one last time from 22 October to 26 January 2026. It can be a blissful experience when you have Neptune in your relationship sector as you lose yourself in love. Alternatively, themes of seduction or betrayal play out.

Before Saturn and Neptune change star sign, there's a deluge of planetary activity in emotional, romantic Pisces, which dominates the first few months of the year. It's potentially one big romantic wave. Firstly, the North Node moves back into Pisces on 12 January where it will remain until 26 July 2026. The nodes are linked to the path of destiny and often coincide with significant turning points in your life. The nodal cycle repeats every 18–19 years and this may be significant for you this year, regarding your relationships, repeating a pattern in your past.

Secondly, your ruling planet Mercury and the planet of love Venus are going back and forth in Pisces, which means they're both in your relationship sector for an unusually long time. Mercury is in Pisces from 14 February to 3 March and again from 30 March to 16 April. Venus is in Pisces from 3 January to 4 February and again from 27 March to 30 April. During this period in the year, both planets will connect with the North Node, Saturn and Neptune in Pisces numerous times. Perhaps, you encounter someone from your past as an old love is awakened. Or you feel able to pursue your sexual or romantic fantasies in a way that you haven't been able to previously.

If you're a typical Virgo, you have a deeply romantic and sexual nature and this could be the time when you have an all-encompassing experience of love. You could be aware of a flood of emotion as you flow between the shores of reality and the waves of fantasy. Just be wary of wearing rose-coloured glasses (Neptune) in a relationship and keep your earthy common sense intact (Saturn). Finding a balance between these two planetary archetypes is essential if you're to move a relationship from the honeymoon phase into a committed partnership.

Perhaps you return to your senses later in the year and reality kicks in. You may be less willing to put love first in September and October, especially if you're asked to give up everything for the one you love. Some adjustments may be necessary in a close relationship. This will be most evident in Virgo season, 22 August to 22 September. This is because you have your planet, Mercury, in Virgo from 2 September to 18 September and the planet of love, Venus, in Virgo from 19 September to 13 October. In all your relationships, this is a time to ensure you're getting your needs met.

SAY YES TO LIFE

Live-wire Uranus is on the move this year as it leaves your fellow earth sign Taurus on 7 July. Uranus returns to Taurus from 8 November to 26 April 2026 and then it's gone. Uranus has been in your fellow earth sign since 2018 and Taurus represents travel and study in your horoscope. It's the bigger picture of life. It's likely that Uranus in Taurus has been encouraging you to say yes to last-minute adventures and be more spontaneous.

Uranus is the freedom planet, a catalyst and innovator. While Uranus is completing its journey through Taurus, you may become an activist fighting for your religion or beliefs. Or you're on a mission to study esoteric texts or explore new learnings. Wherever you're keen to expand your life, physically, intellectually, spiritually or philosophically, make the most of Uranus's journey through your travel and study sector. Uranus teams up with planets in your relationship sector on 4 April and 20 November, ideal dates to book a holiday with a loved one. Or to meet someone new on a study course. Uranus is most active in Taurus season, 19 April to 20 May, and this is when you'll feel Uranus calling you strongly. Uranus aligns with the Sun and Mercury on 17 May and 24 May.

Fast forward to 4 July and there's a Venus–Uranus alliance. Do something special on or around these key dates linked to travel or study and take a leap of faith. Uranus is encouraging you to be spontaneous and say yes to life.

Also this year, you have not one but two New Moons in Virgo, a symbol of new beginnings. This is unusual and exciting. The first New Moon takes place on 23 August, an ideal date to set your intentions for the coming year and plan ahead. This is linked to your personal goals and aims, your image and profile. It's a time to put yourself first and be true to who you are. The second New Moon is a solar eclipse in Virgo on 21 September, the day before the equinox. This can be a powerful time of personal transformation when you see yourself for who you are. You may step into a leadership role, grab your five minutes of fame or become an influencer under these powerful stars. When the eclipses power up your star sign, it can be life changing and you're thrust into the limelight, ready or not. Perhaps this is the year you become an author or a household name because of your writing.

If you're a typical Sun Virgo, you rarely prioritise your own needs, as your nature is to serve and take care of other people. You often become the power behind the throne. Two New Moons in your star sign, one a solar eclipse, are encouraging you to do things differently and take centre stage.

HEALTH AND WELL-BEING

Pluto is god of the underworld in mythology, and the planet linked to power, loss and transformation. Pluto is an extreme and intense energy and it's important to note where Pluto is moving through your horoscope.

In 2023/2024, Pluto started to move back and forth between earth sign Capricorn and air sign Aquarius. These are the play and work sectors of your horoscope. This year, 2025, Pluto is established in Aquarius where it will remain for the next twenty years. Aquarius rules everyday affairs in your horoscope. It's about how you spend your time on a daily basis, through your work and routine. And it's about your lifestyle and health.

This sector of your horoscope is closely aligned with your star sign and this is because you favour a regular routine. Plus, you have an intimate and close relationship with your health and your body. If you're a typical Virgo, you can become obsessed with your health and well-being and eating the right foods for your body. Virgo is linked to the digestive system in the body, so it's right that you pay close attention to what you consume. Health and healing often go hand-in-hand with your mental health and emotional well-being. Pluto's move through Aquarius could intensify this side of your nature. That might be a good thing, i.e. you're on a mission to get fit, strong and healthy. Perhaps you join a gym or take on an intense fitness challenge in 2025. Or you become interested in working in the health industry and become a healer or health practitioner. Wherever Pluto goes, obsession may follow and you're wise to ensure it's a healthy obsession.

As Pluto moves through Aquarius and your lifestyle sector, you may be transforming your regular routine. This is likely to be most intense for you at the start of the year during Aquarius season, 19 January to 18 February. You could have a clear idea of what your 'ideal day' must include. Perhaps, your laser focus is shining a light on being the best you can be and managing your time well. In effect, being an efficient and effective Virgo, key qualities of your star sign.

Pluto's influence can lead to excellence, as long as you're not overly extreme and wear yourself out in the process of optimum fitness or health. This is when you're wise to look to your ruling planet, Mercury. Mercury's nature is flexible and fast, and Mercury's influence keeps you busy. However, three times a year for three weeks at a time, Mercury turns retrograde and slows down. This is a cosmic reminder of how important it is for you, as a Sun Virgo, to schedule in regular breaks and take time out.

This year, Mercury is retrograde from 15 March to 7 April and 9 November to 29 November, both equally positive periods in the year to do less not more. Plus, Mercury's retrograde phase from 18 July to 11 August would be an ideal time to schedule a holiday, a staycation or go on retreat. This is when Mercury is in Leo and the most hidden sector of your horoscope. Mercury remains in Leo for an unusually long time, from 26 June to 2 September. It's an ideal period in the year to take your foot off the accelerator, chill out and kick back. If you could take July and August off work this year, you'd be in tune with your stars. Even if you can't, don't go hell for leather in the middle of the year.

Prioritise your health and well-being, and use the quiet times to calm your anxieties and still your busy mind. Mercury's retrograde phases are a reminder to stop, be quiet and take time out.

RULING PLANET

Your ruling planet is Mercury, linked to communication and the mind. When you follow where Mercury leads, you can make the most of the planet linked to trade, the spoken word, versatility and quick thinking. Use your people skills, your ability to communicate, your gift of the gab. Here's the pattern in 2025:

Up until 9 January: Mercury in Sagittarius – home and family, your past

9 January to 28 January: Mercury in Capricorn – romance, creativity, children

28 January to 14 February: Mercury in Aquarius – work and health

14 February to 3 March: Mercury in Pisces – relationships and contracts

3 March to 30 March: Mercury in Aries – joint finances and taboo issues

30 March to 16 April: Mercury in Pisces – relationships and contracts

16 April to 10 May: Mercury in Aries – joint finances and taboo issues

10 May to 26 May: Mercury in Taurus – travel and study, the bigger picture

26 May to 8 June: Mercury in Gemini – career and vocation

8 June to 26 June: Mercury in Cancer – friendship and groups

26 June to 2 September: Mercury in Leo – hidden sector – retreat, rest, inner work

2 September to 18 September: Mercury in Virgo – your personal goals and aims, image and profile

18 September to 6 October: Mercury in Libra – money, assets, values

6 October to 29 October: Mercury in Scorpio – community and communication

29 October to 19 November: Mercury in Sagittarius – home and family, your past

19 November to 11 December: Mercury in Scorpio – community and communication

11 December onwards: Mercury in Sagittarius – home and family, your past

LUCKY DATES

*Your Full Moon Virgo – eclipse dramas – 14 March

Mercury Aries sextile Jupiter Gemini – 5 May

Mercury conjunct Jupiter Gemini – 8 June

Mercury Virgo sextile Jupiter Cancer – 12 September

Sun conjunct Mercury Virgo – 13 September

Your New Moon Virgo – eclipse power – 21 September

Venus Virgo sextile Jupiter Cancer – 8 October

Mercury Scorpio trine Jupiter Cancer – 6 December

*Eclipses are different to normal Full Moons, as your *2025 Horoscope* will reveal.

LIBRA

YOUR 2025 HOROSCOPE

LIBRA RULERSHIPS

ZODIAC SYMBOL: THE SCALES

RULING PLANET: VENUS, GODDESS OF LOVE, PLANET OF ART AND BEAUTY

MODE/ELEMENT: CARDINAL AIR – MEDIATOR, NEGOTIATOR, EQUAL RIGHTS, PEOPLE PERSON

COLOUR: PASTEL COLOURS

ARCHETYPE: THE DIPLOMAT, THE JUDGE

YOUR TOP TIPS FOR 2025

BECOME A TRAVEL BLOGGER, LINE UP A BIG ADVENTURE

FOLLOW A CHILDHOOD DREAM, START A NEW CAREER

GET SERIOUS ABOUT LOVE, DIVE DEEP INTO A PASSIONATE RELATIONSHIP

LEARN ENERGY WORK, TAKE TIME OUT ON A RETREAT

TRANSFORM YOUR LIFE, YOUR FRIENDSHIPS AND YOUR FINANCES

♎

NEW HORIZONS

The biggest and best planet Jupiter is in your fellow air sign Gemini as the year begins. Jupiter entered Gemini on 25 May 2024 where it remains until 9 June. Wherever Jupiter goes, opportunity and good fortune follow. Therefore, you're wise to make the most of the area of your horoscope where Jupiter resides.

Gemini is the star sign which rules the bigger picture in your horoscope. This may offer you an opportunity to start a new adventure and see new horizons. Jupiter rules travel, study, philosophy, spirituality and any activity that expands your horizons and broadens your experience of life. Jupiter in Gemini emphasises these key themes. You may have a strong desire to live abroad, learn a new language or go to university while Jupiter's in your travel and study sector.

Jupiter is a reminder that luck is an attitude. When you have a big vision, a willingness to take risks, and belief in yourself and what you're doing, then you attract good fortune into your life. Jupiter's move through Gemini could bring a wonderful opportunity to think globally, expand your network and reach out to other people in different countries and cultures. You may want to save the world, as Jupiter's linked to philanthropy and charitable actions. Jupiter rules publishing, the law, truth and justice. Line up some big goals in 2025 and begin your voyage of discovery.

Air signs are active this year as there's major planetary activity taking place in Gemini and Aquarius. The air signs represent networks and connections, they're about ideas and communication, and they represent the visible and invisible ties that bind all of humanity. Your star sign Libra is the third air sign. When planets are in air signs, you often feel in your element. There's a flow in your life as you're pulled or called towards something new.

In 2023/2024, the slowest-moving planet, Pluto, moved in and out of air sign Aquarius. This year, Pluto's established in Aquarius, where it will remain for the next twenty years. Pluto is the planet of power and wherever you find Pluto in your horoscope, it adds intensity and obsession. Aquarius represents the creative sector of your horoscope, the things in life you give birth to. This is about your children, your creative projects, whatever you call 'your baby' – the activities that give you the most pleasure and make you feel the most alive.

Pluto power kicks in early this year and the period from 21 January to 3 February may prove significant. This would be an ideal time to put your natural skills and talents to good use in the world. Set an intention on the New Moon in Aquarius on 29 January to master a skill or turn a hobby into a business. Or perhaps you're on a mission to make children's lives better, either your own children or the children of the world. It can be a big or small mission, what matters is that it's right for you.

Fast forward to 6 April, 5 May and 5 June, and Jupiter's influence is strong. This is when Jupiter in Gemini teams up with the inner planets in Aries and your partnership sector. Look out for a teacher who comes into your life. Or find your double act. As a Sun Libra, you prefer not to go it alone and you are more enthusiastic when you have someone else to team up with. You might go inter-railing with another person. Or set up a joint venture to lead a humanitarian or environmental project. Find the people in your life who can be a great influence on you and your next steps. And offer your services to others in return. Get the flow of reciprocal planetary activity moving and together you're bigger and better.

The stand-out date is arguably a Mercury–Jupiter conjunction in Gemini on 8 June. The planets Mercury and Jupiter are both linked to study and education. You might be accepted for a university place or study course. Perhaps you pass a test or exam. Or you gain new qualifications which enable you to widen your communication reach. Anything which begins under Jupiter's gaze promises success. Say yes to new experiences and plan a big adventure. Events that take place in the first half of the year could help signpost your way forward.

When Jupiter leaves Gemini, this isn't the end of planetary activity in your travel and study sector. Your ruling planet, Venus, moves through Gemini from 4 July to 31 July, an ideal month for a holiday.

More importantly, the planet of change, Uranus, enters Gemini on 7 July. This is a rare shift as it takes Uranus over eighty years to circuit the zodiac. Uranus will remain in Gemini until 8 November and is back next year from 26 April 2026 for the following seven years, until 2032/2033.

Uranus is an exciting planet linked to innovation and invention. It rules technology, which could symbolise an online course or using new technologies to boost your studies. Uranus is especially active on 12 August and 29 August. This is linked to partnership for you. Perhaps you start an internship or you meet someone who introduces you to new ideas and collaborations.

One way or another, life is calling you out to connect with the world, to engage with different cultures and learn about what makes people tick. Explore religion, faith, beliefs – whatever calls you personally.

CAREER AND VOCATION

In 2025, you are being encouraged to turn your gaze towards your future goals and live more expansively. On 9 June, Jupiter enters water sign Cancer and your career and vocation sector, where it remains until 30 June 2026. Cancer is the star sign at the peak of your horoscope. It's about your future path, where you're heading and why. Jupiter's move through Cancer could be spectacular for you, a time when you're at the top of your game.

Think back twelve years to 2013/2014 when Jupiter was last in this same sector of your horoscope. What was happening and how you can learn from events back then? How can you make the most of Jupiter's journey through your career and vocation sector? Jupiter is a symbol of the entrepreneur, the visionary, and Jupiter in Cancer is calling you to play big and step up your game.

Cancer is a caring and kind star sign, so this favours collaboration and a compassionate career or vocational path. You may have a calling to help others and bring people together to benefit from shared experiences. Perhaps you set up a counselling group or a self-help conference or workshop.

Jupiter connects you with the world, as it's the global planet.

Reach out to your wider network to help you expand your career. Plan work abroad or take a sabbatical. It's your choice but the opportunity is there in the coming year, whatever your vision.

There are two stand-out dates that feel exceptionally lucky for your career and vocational goals. These are 24 June and 12 August, when there's a Sun–Jupiter conjunction, followed by a Venus–Jupiter conjunction in Cancer. Both combinations are packed full of opportunity and good fortune, and the Venus–Jupiter conjunction feels especially lucky as Venus is your ruling planet. Do something special on or around these dates. Apply for promotion, set up a business or reach out to a person of influence. Say yes to a new opportunity that could help you get one step closer towards your chosen goal.

Trust your intuition when it comes to your future path. And consider how your past may impact your future or, alternatively, how family connections could influence your future success. Relevant dates here could be 22 June, 12 September and 8 October. Someone from your past could be the person to open doors for you. Or the cycle of karma kicks in and you're repaid for what you've given out previously.

Jupiter's move through Cancer is a reminder that kindness and caring are important values to bring into the workplace. If you work in an industry that's hard-nosed or materialistic, it's even more important to highlight people power and the validity of emotional intelligence and heart-felt connections.

Later in the year, there's a flow between planets in Scorpio and your money sector and Cancer and your career sector. The key dates are 24 October, 28 October, 17 November, 26 November and 6 December. These combinations could prove lucrative, and a new job, role or opportunity pays well. The only proviso is that Mercury is retrograde from 9 November to 29 November. Use this period to review your situation and rethink your strategy rather than sign and seal a deal. When Mercury turns direct at the end of November, this is the best time to ask for what you want, especially around money.

There is one period in the year when you're wise to be careful whom you get involved with. The dates to note are 15 June to 19 June. Perhaps a partner is disapproving of your career path. Or there's someone in your life who could tarnish your reputation if you get involved with them. It depends on your personal situation how this might play out for you. Be aware that not everyone will have your best interests at heart during this period in the year.

As 2025 begins, you may not feel optimistic about your next steps. This has a lot to do with action planet Mars retrograde in Cancer, your career and future sector, from 6 January to 24 February. This can be a time when things don't work out the way you want them to. Life may step in to slow you down or you're reconsidering your long-term options.

Use the timing of astrology to know when to make your move. Be assertive when Mars is back up to speed in Cancer from 24 February to 18 April. And get in step with the flow of success once lucky Jupiter is moving through Cancer, your career and vocation sector.

This isn't a year to hold back on your long-term dreams or cherished goals. Jupiter's encouraging you to embrace your career and vocational plans wholeheartedly. Whether this means enjoying your freedom or bringing people together to create a better world, do what's right for you.

RELATIONSHIPS AND COMMITMENT

In 2025, the planet of commitment, Saturn, enters Aries and your relationship sector for the first time in almost thirty years. Saturn moves into Aries on 25 May, where it remains until 1 September. Saturn returns to Aries on 14 February 2026 and will be in your opposite star sign until April 2028. This means that commitment and responsibility will play an integral role in your close relationships and your one-to-ones. Wherever you find Saturn in your horoscope, this is an area of your life where you're wise to work hard and where lessons can be learned.

Sometimes a relationship comes to an end under Saturn's gaze. There can be a 'commit or quit' theme playing out. If you're in a long-term relationship or marriage, turn your attention towards love. Some bonds and ties will grow stronger under Saturn's gaze and you're being asked to be more decisive. If you're a typical Sun Libra, it takes you a while to make up your mind and you can be indecisive. Saturn's move through your relationship zone may demand a new way of doing things. Assert yourself where necessary and don't let anyone else tell you what you can and can't do. Ensure firm boundaries are in place in love, to keep everyone happy.

Saturn's move through Aries is a different vibe to what's been happening recently in your relationship sector. This is linked to the eclipse cycle that's been cutting across the Aries/Libra axis of the zodiac. This is an important eclipse cycle for you, as it focuses on your star sign Libra and your relationship star sign Aries. This eclipse cycle began in April 2023 and completes in March 2025. Eclipses often coincide with the highs and lows of life. They can be a time of accelerated growth, coinciding with drama or crisis. Relationships can end or begin during this eclipse cycle.

The final eclipse takes place on 29 March and it's a New Moon solar eclipse in Aries. Solar eclipses represent turbo-powered new beginnings. However, they sometimes emerge from an ending. Notice who comes into your life on or around this powerful eclipse or what significant event plays out. Whoever you meet could play an important role in your life moving forward. However, you're wise to be patient as the eclipse falls during a double retrograde phase. This involves your ruling planet, Venus, and the planet of communication, Mercury.

Venus spends an unusually long time in Aries, your relation-ship sector, this year – from 4 February to 27 March and again from 30 April to 6 June. This planet/sign combination favours passionate encounters. Though, when planets are in your oppo-site star sign, this isn't only about love as it includes all your one-to-one relationships – i.e. this could be about a business partnership, a coaching or teaching relationship. It might be a time when you're considering a joint venture. Or you're keen to team up with another person for accountability or boosting your chances of success.

Venus's retrograde phase takes place from 2 March to 13 April. For forty days and forty nights, Venus journeys into the under-world, and this is a time of inner learning and personal revelation. Alternatively, you're involved in an on-off relation-ship. Or you and your partner are spending time apart. Sometimes there's a chance to rejuvenate an old relationship or an ex comes back into your life. If you have strong feelings for someone in your past, this can be a positive time to explore those feelings once again. As long as you put off making a major decision until Venus turns direct.

What Venus retrograde is good for is to turn your attention inwards. You may be reflecting about love, what love means to you, whether you're in the right relationship, what sort of relationship you want. Use the Venus retrograde phase to focus more intensely on passion and desire.

A significant date is 23 March, when the Sun illuminates Venus in Aries. This combination can be revelatory and insightful. It's the mid-way point of the Venus retrograde phase and, for the next twenty days, Venus is gathering strength. It turns direct and will emerge as a morning star, embodying its warrior archetype on 13 April. This is an important turning point when the truth comes to light. Alternatively, you know your own mind or you find out what someone else wants. Use this switch in direction to take action.

Another major planet moving into Aries is Neptune, the planet linked to romance, dreams and the imagination. Neptune enters Aries on 30 March, where it remains until 22 October. Neptune will return to Aries on 26 January 2026, until 2038/2039. Neptune is a romantic influence. Although, you're wise not to wear rose-tinted glasses when it comes to love, as Neptune can represent seduction and betrayal.

This year, Saturn and Neptune are working together in Aries. These two planets are opposites as Saturn represents reality and commitment, while Neptune represents fantasy and escapism. In June, July and August, the two planets are side by side, preparing for their rare conjunction, which takes place in February 2026. Ideally, you want to find a balance between the two planetary energies, to keep love real and turn dreams into reality.

Be wary of becoming gloomy and disillusioned around love, especially if you're single and you've given up on love. Or perhaps you're in a relationship with a partner who's undergoing an existential crisis. Try not to give in to fear or doubt, and don't allow guilt to seep into your close relationships.

Ultimately, Saturn and Neptune favour combining commitment and romance within a relationship. They encourage an act of surrender to love and to life.

Also this year, Pluto is moving through Aquarius, the sector of your horoscope linked to romance and love affairs. Pluto is an intense and obsessive planetary energy, encouraging you to dive deep into your passions. However, Pluto can negate what it touches. This could symbolise the end of an on-off love affair. Or perhaps you make a decision alongside your partner that you're not going to have children. You could make some extreme decisions with Pluto in Aquarius.

One way or another, 2025 is likely to be an exciting and passionate year for love and relationships. It's not straightforward, however, and love is invariably complex. Yet, you're being invited to be true to your Libra archetype and prioritise your love relationships.

LIFESTYLE AND HEALTH

In 2025, Saturn and Neptune are starting to complete their journeys through Pisces and your work, service and health sector. As they shift star signs, you may feel their energy strongly.

Saturn has been in Pisces since March 2023. It leaves Pisces on 25 May and returns from 1 September to 14 February 2026. Neptune has been in Pisces since 2012. It leaves Pisces on 30 March and returns from 22 October to 26 January 2026. Saturn in your work and health sector can make life hard going. You're working too hard, you find work boring or you experience a period of unemployment.

The plus side of Saturn is being committed to your work and health. You may enjoy the security of the nine-to-five. Or you're developing healthy habits and you're a regular gym-goer or yoga devotee. You may be exploring your own healing abilities, or be interested in reiki or energy work.

Saturn remains in Pisces until the end of May and Pisces' energy is in full flow in the first few months of the year. On 12 January, the North Node moves into Pisces, where it remains until 26 July 2026. The pull of the nodes can feel karmic and you may have a strong sense of the call of destiny. Perhaps, you're ready to lead a healthy lifestyle or you want to become a volunteer and tread a new path in life.

As 2025 gets underway, your planet Venus is also in Pisces, a nod towards prioritising the areas of work, service and health. Venus is in Pisces from 3 January to 4 February and again from 27 March to 30 April. Plus, talk planet Mercury is in Pisces from 14 February to 3 March, and again from 30 March to 16 April. This favours health and lifestyle collaborations, teamwork and the flow of ideas and information.

Both planets will be retrograde in Pisces in March and April, an ideal time to go on retreat. You may be drawn back towards the past or be called to return to a place you've been before that was meaningful for you. Wherever you are, ensure you create the time and space in your life to rest and relax.

As Venus and Mercury move back and forth through Pisces, they connect with the North Node, Saturn and Neptune in a flow of energy. Pisces is a boundless star sign, vast and endless like the sea. This is about life beyond the everyday, calling you to listen to the universe. Trust your intuition and dive deep into nature's bounty and its healing energies.

The nodes are linked to the eclipses. This year's major eclipse cycle cuts across the Virgo/Pisces axis of the zodiac. These are the sectors of your horoscope linked to work and health, service to others and devotion to a higher purpose. This eclipse cycle began in September 2024 and completes in February 2027. This year, there are two Full Moon lunar eclipses on 14 March and 7 September. These periods in the year are likely to be pivotal for you. Perhaps you're the one who's keen to turn things around or you receive a life shock that awakens you to the possibility of doing things differently.

There may be a sense of urgency around inner work or personal healing. Yes, you may be called to serve others this year, but heal the healer first. Take time out for yourself when needed.

Later this year, there are two New Moons in Virgo, which is unusual. Virgo is the most private sector of your horoscope, an ideal time to focus on self-care and caring for others. The first New Moon takes place on 23 August. The second New Moon takes place on 21 September, the day before the equinox and it's a solar eclipse. This is a powerful portal of energy. You may take time out from your usual routine in September. Or perhaps you're studying, doing research or turning away from the outside world. This can be when you benefit from quiet time, prayer or solitude. Don't lose yourself trying to deal with what's happening elsewhere. Too much going on and this could lead to overwhelm.

Eclipses are often dramatic. Sometimes, you sense that things have to fall apart before they can be rebuilt. Try not to let any worry or anxiety take hold during eclipse season. Learn to slow down more and trust in life.

When your ruling planet, Venus, moves through Virgo from 19 September to 13 October, put your needs first. Then, when Venus moves through your star sign Libra from 13 October to 6 November, you'll have a better idea of how to bring more balance and harmony into your everyday life.

MONEY MATTERS

Live-wire Uranus changes star sign this year and is starting to complete its journey through Taurus and your joint finance sector, where it has been since 2018. Uranus is in Taurus up until 7 July and again from 8 November to 26 April 2026.

As Uranus rules unpredictability, Uranus's journey through Taurus could coincide with extra expense or extra earnings. Uranus is the planet of highs and lows, and its volatile energy can play out either way. Perhaps your financial situation has been more unstable over the last few years. You aren't totally free of Uranus's shocks and surprises in 2025, but you can start to make the right moves for you.

Uranus is active during Taurus's season, which coincides with the most abundant and fertile period in the northern hemisphere. The Sun moves through Taurus from 19 April to 20 May. There are two powerful Uranus conjunctions on 17 May and 24 May. These dates could be decisive for you, when you're ready to take a risk and leap into a new financial situation. Also, your planet, Venus, is moving through Taurus from 6 June to 4 July. Taurus rules all forms of financial transactions, such as mortgages, inheritance, investments, savings, debt, loans and benefits. This is a positive period to focus on finances and look at ways of boosting your personal situation.

On 4 July, the day that Venus is preparing to leave Taurus, there's a lively Venus–Uranus conjunction. Venus and Uranus can work well together, encouraging you to leap into action, take a risk and use your charm and diplomacy to attract good fortune into your life. In addition, Uranus in Taurus connects with planets in Pisces and your work sector on 4 April and 20 November. Both times Mercury is retrograde, so this could be about something hidden that comes to light. You might be offered a job behind closed doors. Or hear about a money-making opportunity that you could fit around your current job or routine. Wait for Mercury to turn direct on 7 April and 29 November respectively to make your move.

The last few months of the year could prove lively for money matters. This is because the inner planets all move through Scorpio and your personal money sector. Action planet Mars is first from 22 September to 4 November. Use this period in the year to be assertive when it comes to money.

Your ruling planet Venus joins the Sun and talk planet Mercury in Scorpio from 6 November to 30 November. However, this is when Mercury is retrograde, from 9 November to 29 November. Therefore, there's a theme of secrecy or keeping your cards close to your chest. It may be a time when you're having to safeguard your finances.

Also, there are oppositions from Uranus to the inner planets in Scorpio on the following dates: 19 November, 21 November, 30 November and 10 December. These aren't the best dates to take a risk. Uranus's oppositions can prove challenging and you may be caught up in a conflict situation or be up against tough opposition.

However, you have Jupiter on your side during the same period. Jupiter in Cancer, your career sector, teams up with planets in Scorpio on 24 October, 28 October, 17 November, 26 November and 6 December. These are better dates for making a financial move, as long as you avoid the Mercury retrograde phase.

Play your cards right towards the end of the year and you could do well come December. This may be linked to a new money-earning opportunity that pulls you out into the world.

FRIENDS AND FAMILY

If you're a typical Libra, you have a wide social circle. You're one of the social air signs and people are important to you. This year, you may experience some changes within your friendships. This may be linked to what's happening with the inner planets as they move through Leo and your friendship and group sector.

As 2025 begins, action planet Mars is retrograde in Leo until 6 January. You may have fallen out with a friend over the festive period. If this is true for you, you're wise to wait until Mars turns direct on 24 February to heal any rift.

Mars is back in Leo in direct motion from 18 April to 17 June, a positive period for being assertive around friendship and group activities. Talk planet Mercury spends an unusually long time in Leo and your friendship and group sector from 26 June to 2 September.

Why are friendships under the cosmic spotlight during the middle of the year? Perhaps you're holidaying with friends or you have a lot of social events lined up. Alternatively, you may be immersed with a new group. Perhaps you're on a retreat or you join in a group activity that's about personal transformation.

You may be involved in keeping a group alive or active during this period in the year. Be a voice for the people, start a campaign and be true to your beliefs and ideologies.

Yet, Leo is where Mercury turns retrograde from 18 July to 11 August. This can be a time of misunderstandings, so wait for Mercury to turn direct before reaching out and reconnecting. This can be the time that new information comes to light.

Your planet, Venus, is the last of the inner planets to move through Leo, from 25 August to 19 September. This is a lovely period in the year to arrange a get-together with friends or throw a party or social event.

Venus was retrograde in Leo in the middle of 2023 and you may be aware that your friendships have been changing and developing since then. If so, this process continues this year. And if you're on a personal journey to find your authentic self, this will no doubt impact your friendships. Acknowledge how far you've come and recognise the friends you want to be around and spend more time with. They're the ones who give you something back and it's not just about taking from you. This is a powerful year to develop the right friendships and find the right group where you can be true to yourself, at the same time as having fun.

Also, you may be aware of a deep shift that's taken place within your family or linked to your past. In 2023/2024, power planet Pluto completed its journey through Capricorn and the star sign at the base of your horoscope. This isn't an easy journey for Pluto. You may have encountered loss or death. Perhaps secrets from the past were revealed.

Whatever's true for you, in 2025 you can close a door on the past. It may feel as if you've shed a skin, like the snake, and you're moving forward with a sense of renewal or rebirth. This year's astrology is calling you to keep moving forward and, whether literally or metaphorically, leave the past behind.

RULING PLANET

Knowing where your ruling planet Venus is moving through your horoscope can help you plan accordingly. Venus is the planet linked to attraction, popularity and pleasure. Which areas of your life does Venus light up? Here's the pattern:

Up until 3 January: Venus in Aquarius – romance, creativity, children, fun

3 January to 4 February: Venus in Pisces – work and lifestyle

4 February to 27 March: Venus in Aries – relationships and contracts

27 March to 30 April: Venus in Pisces – work and lifestyle

30 April to 6 June: Venus in Aries – relationships and contracts

6 June to 4 July: Venus in Taurus – joint finances and shared resources

4 July to 31 July: Venus in Gemini – travel and study, the bigger picture

31 July to 25 August: Venus in Cancer – career and vocation

25 August to 19 September: Venus in Leo – friendship and groups

19 September to 13 October: Venus in Virgo – retreat, rest, inner work

13 October to 6 November: Venus in Libra – your personal goals and aims, image and profile

6 November to 30 November: Venus in Scorpio – money matters

30 November to 24 December: Venus in Sagittarius – community and communication

24 December onwards: Venus in Capricorn – home and family, your past

LUCKY DATES

Sun Aquarius trine Jupiter Gemini – 30 January

Mars turns direct in Cancer – 24 February

Your Full Moon Libra – achievement/culmination – 13 April

Venus Aries sextile Jupiter Gemini – 5 June

Venus conjunct Jupiter Cancer – 12 August

Venus Virgo sextile Jupiter Cancer – 8 October

Your New Moon Libra – new beginnings – 21 October

Venus Scorpio trine Jupiter Cancer – 26 November

SCORPIO

YOUR 2025 HOROSCOPE

SCORPIO RULERSHIPS

ZODIAC SYMBOL: THE SCORPION

RULING PLANET: TRADITIONAL – MARS,
GOD OF WAR; MODERN – PLUTO,
GOD OF THE UNDERWORLD

MODE/ELEMENT: FIXED WATER – DEEP,
INTENSE, OBSESSIVE, LASER FOCUS

COLOUR: BLACK, BLOOD RED

ARCHETYPE: THE PHOENIX,
THE DETECTIVE

YOUR TOP TIPS FOR 2025

PLAY THE STOCK MARKET,
BOOST YOUR WEALTH

PLAN A BIG TRIP, EXPAND
YOUR PHILOSOPHY OF LIFE

GIVE UP AN ADDICTION,
LEAD A HEALTHY LIFESTYLE

SAY YES TO ROMANCE, ENLIVEN
YOUR LOVE RELATIONSHIPS

RECALIBRATE THE WORK/LIFE BALANCE

♏

FINANCES AND GOOD FORTUNE

Jupiter is the planet to take note of when you want to know where opportunity lies. This is because Jupiter is the best planet in astrology, linked to growth and expansion, luck and good fortune. As 2025 begins, Jupiter is in air sign Gemini. Jupiter moved into Gemini on 25 May 2024, where it remains until 9 June.

Gemini rules joint finances and shared resources in your horoscope. This includes all forms of financial transactions – e.g. loans, mortgages, tax, investments, inheritance, savings and debt. You find many Scorpios working on the financial trading floors and in the money markets. And, when Jupiter's in Gemini, you may receive a gift or bonus; you could boost your financial portfolio or increase your wealth. It's also the perfect time to get expert advice, especially when it comes to finances or legal matters. Jupiter is a global planet so think big. You're being encouraged to expand your circle of expertise.

In your horoscope, Gemini represents the hidden and taboo issues in life, including money, power, sex, death and the cycle of life, rebirth and renewal. This is where you find the mysteries of life and, if you're a typical Scorpio, this will resonate with you. This can play out for you in different ways. For example, you may love reading thrillers or the colour black; you're into esotericism or secret hidden knowledge. Perhaps you have a spirit guide or visit psychics regularly; you're obsessed with near-death experiences or work with the dying.

As Jupiter moves through Gemini, expand your learning and your thirst for knowledge. Gemini is one of the air signs which rules the spoken and written word. This may enhance your passion of discovering new experiences through podcasts, books or teachings.

Yet, Jupiter in Gemini favours practical money management too. From 19 January, the focus is on the air sign Aquarius ruling your home and family. Jupiter teams up with key planets in Aquarius on 30 January and 3 February. This would be an ideal time to apply for a mortgage, sort out your family finances or deal with an inheritance.

Fast forward to 6 April, 5 May and 5 June, and the inner planets team up with Jupiter in Gemini as they move through Aries and your work and health sector. These dates may be good ones on which to apply for a job or find the right health practitioner. Invest in your learning and well-being.

The stand-out date while Jupiter's in Gemini is arguably 8 June, when there's a Mercury–Jupiter conjunction. Both planets are linked to education and study, and this would be an ideal date to attend or run a workshop.

Finances feel lucky during this period in the year. There could be a celebration, a promotion or an opportunity to boost your cash flow, your investments or clear a debt. Work along-side other people to get the best returns.

Jupiter leaves Gemini on 9 June but this isn't the end of lively activity in your joint finance sector. Think of this period as setting yourself up for the future. Focus on your money mindset. Change your thought patterns and you'll attract more abundance into your life.

On 4 July, the second best planet, Venus, enters Gemini and, a few days later, on 7 July, there's another significant planetary shift. This involves the planet of innovation, Uranus, moving into Gemini, where it will remain until 8 November. Uranus will return to Gemini next year on 26 April 2026 and remains in your joint finance sector for the following seven years. This is a potential game changer and, wherever Uranus goes, things can happen fast. This is encouraging you to change the way you think about money. Perhaps the time is right to break free from a financial tie that no longer serves you.

Uranus isn't a stable influence in your joint finance sector, however. It favours freedom over responsibility, and is more likely to relate to highs and lows than regular, steady earnings. Your willingness to take financial risks could reach stratospheric levels in the years to come.

Uranus connects with key planets in your work sector on 12 August and 29 August. This might be when you can nail a deal or sign a contract.

Uranus in Gemini is likely to increase your interest in life after death, the occult and the great mysteries of life. But Uranus is also future-oriented and linked to new age and technological advancements. Therefore, it's imperative that you keep up-to-date with new financial trends and look at innovative ways of boosting your wealth.

Your ruling planet, Mars, enters Sagittarius and your personal money sector a few days before Uranus leaves Gemini on 8 November. This may be when you can put what you've learned into practice. Mars remains in Sagittarius until 15 December. However, be aware that Mercury turns retrograde in Sagittarius on 9 November. Mercury retrograde is often a topsy-turvy time for the money markets. It's the planet which lends its name to market and merchandise. Wait until 29 November when Mercury turns direct before leaping into action.

Throughout November, do your research and rethink your next steps. Then, be proactive and make your move. You might be able to take advantage of swiftly moving financial trends. Focus on finances in 2025 and set yourself up for a prosperous financial future.

STUDY AND FOREIGN CONNECTIONS

Jupiter enters your fellow water sign Cancer on 9 June, where it will remain until 30 June 2026. Cancer is your travel and study sector and an area of your horoscope in which Jupiter feels at home. This is because Jupiter rules travel, study, philosophy, spirituality and any activity that expands your horizons and broadens your experience of life. It's about the bigger picture and looking to the future. If you want to travel abroad or live in another country, if you want to take a sabbatical from work and explore a new direction, it starts with believing and knowing that anything's possible.

Set your intentions as Jupiter's year of exploration begins and let the universe hear your voice. Jupiter moves into Cancer in the run-up to Cancer season, 21 June to 22 July. This would be a wonderful time in the year to plan a holiday or sign up to a new course. There are two powerful conjunctions taking place in Cancer on 24 June and 12 August. The first is a Sun–Jupiter conjunction and the second is a Venus–Jupiter conjunction, and these will be two of the luckiest dates this year.

Think globally, expand your network and reach out to other

people in different countries and cultures. You may want to save the world as Jupiter is closely linked to philanthropy and charitable actions. Jupiter also rules publishing, the law, truth and humanity, so stake your claim and begin your voyage of discovery. The cosmic spotlight is turning towards your long-term goals, making it an ideal time to line up some new adventures for the year ahead and beyond. Jupiter in Cancer is encouraging you to discover your purpose and what gives your life meaning.

Cancer is an emotional water sign, like your star sign, Scorpio. Therefore, this is about connections too, not only your interests. This is confirmed because of the planetary aspects Jupiter is making while moving through Cancer. On 22 June, 12 September and 8 October, Jupiter aligns with key planets in Virgo and your friendship and group sector. These would be ideal dates to plan a holiday with friends, or sign up for a group experience and join in with others on a journey of learning or self-development. It's not just about having fun, as these are caring combinations. Perhaps, you choose to volunteer for an organisation that takes you abroad. Or you're involved in a charity fundraising event that helps people around the world. It's likely that whatever you get involved in, you're taking on a leading role. This is because Jupiter in Cancer teams up with planets moving through your star sign towards the end of this year.

The key dates are 24 October, 28 October, 17 November, 26 November and 6 December. These are lucky dates on which to explore your foreign connections and pursue your long-term goals and dreams. Plus, your ruling planet Mars is in Scorpio from 22 September to 4 November. This only happens once every two years. It gives you extra drive and ambition to move forward with your personal goals and aims. This isn't a time of the year to hold back. Instead, dive deep into your passions and engage actively and fully with life and the world.

You may be learning about new philosophies or be teaching hidden mysteries. You might decide to retrain to become a lawyer or human rights advocate. You could get your book published in different languages around the world. Or be exploring a new religion.

As 2025 begins, however, you may not have faith that you're on the right path. This is because your planet Mars moves back into Cancer on 6 January and remains retrograde until 24 February. This indicates that there's no need to rush into things as the year begins. Instead, you're wise to explore your options and plan your strategy for your next steps. Sometimes, when your ruling planet is retrograde, you're not in charge or in control. Things don't work out the way you want them to, you're low on energy and you have to take a slow pace.

Mars travelled through Cancer from 4 September to 4 November 2024. Therefore, this may be linked to what you were planning during this period. Perhaps, you were on track but got diverted. Once Mars turns direct on 24 February, you may find you have strength or courage to press ahead with your chosen goals. Mars remains in Cancer until 18 April.

If you're travelling or planning a big trip this year, you're in sync with your stars. It's an excellent year to invest in a study course or learning programme. Explore your beliefs, your philosophy on life, your spiritual path. Push back the boundaries of what's possible, and aim for unity and togetherness within the world.

LIFESTYLE AND HEALTH

The planet of responsibility and commitment, Saturn, changes star sign this year. From 25 May to 1 September, Saturn is in fire sign Aries and your work and health sector. Saturn will return to Aries on 14 February 2026 and remain here until April 2028.

Saturn represents endings and commitments. A job or contract could come to an end under these stars. Or perhaps you commit to a project for the next couple of years. What you're wise to be careful of when Saturn is in Aries is that you don't turn into a workaholic, put duty before pleasure or become a harsh task-master. If you're a typical Scorpio, there's a side to your nature that's driven and you often give 100 per cent and more.

Keep close tabs on your health while Saturn's in Aries to ensure that your stress levels don't rise to an unacceptable level. This may happen when your ruling planet, Mars, opposes Saturn on 9 August. This combination can push you to the limit.

Aries is ruled by Mars, your traditional ruling planet, and you may need to watch your anger, frustration or irritation while Saturn's in Aries. If you're bored of what you're doing or you're dealing with difficult customers, this could take its toll.

Aim to manage your time efficiently and effectively while Saturn's in Aries. Use your organisational skills to stay on top of whatever comes your way. And if you can work more from home, this could benefit you.

Regarding your health, this would be an ideal time to hone your self-discipline and put some new habits in place that benefit your mind, body and soul. You may already have experienced some shocks around your lifestyle and the work/life balance in recent years. This is because of the eclipse cycle cutting across the Aries/Libra axis of the zodiac. This started in April 2023 and will complete in March this year. Eclipses coincide with change, wherever they fall in your horoscope. This is about the work/life balance for you, knowing when to push ahead and give your all, and when to stop and slow down.

Sometimes, there's a drama or a crisis which forces you to take stock and do things differently. In 2023/2024, there were two New Moon solar eclipses in Aries. Solar eclipses are like turbo-powered New Moons which accelerate growth. On 29 March, there's a third and final solar eclipse in Aries, your work and health sector. This may be a time when you're getting physically fit and strong. You might decide to train for a marathon, start using weights or apply for a new physical job or role on the back of this powerful eclipse. Alternatively, life may step in, to show you where change is required.

During this period in the year, there are two retrograde phases taking place. On 2 March, the planet of relating, Venus, turns retrograde in Aries. And on 15 March, communication planet Mercury turns retrograde also in Aries. Perhaps, a job or contract comes to an end during this period in the year. Alternatively, it would be an ideal period to take some time out from your everyday routine and give yourself the space to explore what's next. Go on a retreat, prioritise your health and well-being and tune in to the rhythm and flow of nature.

Venus is the planet linked to women in your horoscope and you could connect more deeply with the divine feminine during the forty-day retrograde phase. This is an important period in the year to recharge your batteries and, if necessary, to rest and retreat. The Venus retrograde phase from 2 March to 13 April coincides with Lent, traditionally a time to give something up in the Christian tradition. You could commit to a period of fasting or cut sugar or alcohol out of your diet, whatever works for you. Use this period in the year to recalibrate your mind, body and soul.

There's another major planet moving into Aries this year – Neptune, one of the slower-moving generational planets. Neptune enters Aries on 30 March, where it remains until 22 October. Neptune will return to Aries on 26 January 2026 and be in your work and health sector until 2038/39.

In June, July and August this year, Saturn and Neptune are side by side. This is the preparation for an epic Saturn/Neptune conjunction in Aries in February 2026. This is the first time these two planets will come together since 1989. It's an unusual pairing, as Saturn represents hard work and reality, whereas Neptune represents daydreaming and fantasy. Ideally, you want these two planets working together and there is a spiritual aspect to both Saturn and Neptune: Saturn is the shaman and Neptune is where you seek bliss and transcendence in life.

If you're a typical Scorpio, you're interested in esotericism and recognise the power of intention, meditation and yoga. Saturn and Neptune in Aries may increase your desire to escape the everyday and routine side of life, to seek oneness or a spiritual connection.

Neptune in Aries is a reminder to bring compassion and caring into everything you do. This sector of your horoscope rules service to others. Therefore, you may choose to offer your skills in a volunteering role. Aries rules employees, lodgers and pets. You could become involved in animal welfare or step into a role looking after the well-being of your fellow employees.

Be wary of pushing back the boundaries of life too far and losing yourself in a way that's unhealthy or unhelpful. You might become aware of your addictions. Or make a radical choice to go teetotal and cut toxicity out of your diet. Don't let fear or guilt kick in, however, and learn to love yourself and be kind and caring to yourself too. Put new and healthy habits and daily practices in place, which keep you anchored and attached to life in a positive way.

LOVE AND CONNECTIONS

The planet of change Uranus is completing its journey through Taurus and your relationship sector this year and next. In 2025, Uranus leaves your opposite star sign, Taurus, from 7 July to 8 November. Uranus finally departs your relationship sector in April 2026.

Uranus is the planet of sudden happenings, shocks and surprises, and it has been in Taurus since 2018. You may have been impulsive in love. Or perhaps you've come into contact with people whose behaviour or actions have been unpredictable. Uranus is the classic divorce planet as it rules splits, as well as out-of-the-blue lightning bolt strikes of love. It's both an exciting and potentially disruptive planetary archetype.

Uranus kicks in again this year and is lively on 17 May, 24 May and on 4 July. These are dates when anything goes when it comes to love. If you're a typical Scorpio, you tend to dive in deep on an emotional level and you are often led by your libido and your passion. Alternatively, you could shock others with your actions by making an unusual love choice. Or perhaps external events bring change to a current partnership or marriage, requiring the two of you to adjust your expectations.

Romance is there for the taking this year, which has a lot to do with Saturn and Neptune completing their journeys through

Pisces and your romance sector. Pisces rules love affairs, children and pregnancy in your horoscope. It's the things in life you 'give birth to'. Saturn, however, isn't a particularly romantic influence. While Saturn's been in Pisces since March 2023, you may have experienced a love drought. Or perhaps it played out as a creative block or issues regarding children or pregnancy. Alternatively, you may have committed to romance, been a disciplined parent in a good way, or perhaps you've found the self-discipline to learn a hobby or finesse a creative project.

As Saturn completes its journey through Pisces up until 25 May, it's not alone. For starters, romantic Neptune is in Pisces until 30 March. Yet there's more peak planetary activity taking place in this sector of your horoscope. On 12 January, the North Node enters Pisces, where it remains until 26 July 2026. The nodes are linked to the path of destiny as the wheel of fortune turns and fate kicks in. If you're looking for love, the start of 2025 could coincide with a huge love affair.

This theme is intensified because the planet of love Venus is in Pisces from 3 January to 4 February. And talk planet Mercury is in Pisces from 14 February to 3 March. This is a gorgeous period of the year in which to line up some romantic dates.

As Venus and Mercury move through Pisces, they trigger the North Node, Saturn and Neptune. It's a romantic Pisces overload which could coincide with falling in love, one of the ways you 'lose yourself'.

It's not just about love, however, but your connection with your creative or spiritual source. Where are the waves rolling in? Where are your emotions pulling you? Use this emotive astrology in a good way.

Mercury and Venus are both retrograde from March into April and both planets turn direct in Pisces – Mercury on 7 April and Venus on 13 April. This is the time to make up your mind about love, to reach out and reconnect. It's deep and powerful astrology, a yearning or a calling.

Diving deep into the emotional realm, whether through romance, creativity or spirituality, isn't always an easy path if you lose your way. Keep coming back to yourself and stay connected to the earth and to your friends. This is a key feature of the Virgo/Pisces eclipse cycle, which began in September 2024 and will continue until February 2027. This eclipse cycle highlights the social axis of your horoscope. It's linked to friends and group activities, society and politics, also children and lovers. These are the areas of accelerated growth, where change may happen and fast.

There are two powerful Full Moon lunar eclipses: one in Virgo on 14 March and one in Pisces on 7 September. Emotions are heightened during Full Moon eclipses and they often coincide with dramatic events. During eclipses, what's hidden can come to light. It's not a time to overreact. Instead, wait a few days for the eclipse energy to settle before responding or making any major decisions.

You may realise that your emotional needs are changing during the coming year and this impacts your friendships and group associations. Love and friendship could lead you astray. Yet, the truer you are to yourself in 2025 and the more you open your heart, the more likely you are to attract the right people into your life.

HOME AND PAST

As a Scorpio, your co-ruler is Pluto, one of the generational modern planets. Pluto adds intensity and obsession to your Scorpio nature and is the planet of power and transformation. You may already be aware of the importance of using power to good effect.

In 2023/2024, Pluto changed star sign and this is a hugely significant shift. This doesn't happen very often and Pluto won't change star sign again for the next twenty years. Pluto left behind Capricorn and your communication sector last year, where it had been since 2008, and entered Aquarius, your home and family sector. This is the star sign at the base of your horoscope. Pluto is now firmly established in Aquarius and you may already be aware of how Pluto is transforming the roots of your life.

Perhaps you're on a mission to buy your own home or start your own family. Pluto can pull you back to the past too, whether secrets emerge or you're dealing with inheritance or past legacies. You may step into a leadership role within the collective or your community. You might return to the place of your birth or your homeland. Or perhaps you feel empowered to explore your past in a way that's healing and deeply transformative.

While Pluto's in Aquarius, you could become a property investor, build your own home or get involved in community living. You might become a soul midwife and work with the dying. Or become an advocate of Swedish death cleaning. One of your zodiac symbols is the phoenix, who rises from the ashes. And Pluto's journey through Aquarius could connect you more deeply with the cycle of life, death, rebirth and renewal. The base of the horoscope is sometimes termed 'the womb and the tomb', where life begins and where life ends. With Pluto in Aquarius, your role may be to help create a better understanding of the individual's journey beyond the physical plane.

Aquarius season runs from 19 January to 18 February. It's this key period in the year when you may have a strong sense of how Pluto is playing out in your life. The time from 21 January to 3 February is pivotal. You may have a strong urge or desire to get things right in the home and family areas of your life.

Plus, the air signs Gemini and Aquarius are foreground in 2025 and over the coming years. This is about your financial future and your security. It's about funding your own life and ensuring that the lives of others, your family and loved ones, are safe and secure. Turn Pluto's laser focus towards improving these key areas of your life.

FUTURE PATH

Pluto is calling you back towards the past – this is the opposite end of the axis of the zodiac calling you forth into the future. Pluto is moving through Aquarius at the base of your horoscope, while all the inner planets will be moving through Leo and your career and future sector at different times throughout the year.

Leo is the star sign at the peak of your horoscope. This is an area of your life in which there have been some significant stops and starts since the middle of 2023. This is because all of the inner planets, Venus, Mars and Mercury, have turned retrograde in Leo and your career and future sector, potentially slowing you down or stopping you in your tracks. This is an interesting pattern, as it suggests that you may have been changing your mind regarding your career or future path. Retrograde planets turn your attention inwards and they're about inner change. When you change on the inside – i.e. your values, your faith, your mindset – this is what can create change on the outside and your path in life. This is important to note because, as 2025 begins, your ruling planet Mars is retrograde in Leo. Mars turned retrograde here on 6 December 2024 and Mars remains retrograde in Leo until 6 January. This may be significant that you have your ruling planet in reverse motion in Leo and your future sector as the year is beginning.

Traditionally, the start of the year is an ideal time to set your New Year's resolutions and look ahead to the future. However, this isn't true for you and you're wise to use the timing of your astrology to good effect. As the year begins, your two ruling planets, Mars and Pluto, are in opposition, cutting across the foundations of your horoscope on 3 January. This suggests that you're being pulled back into the past. Perhaps this is connected to your parents, your childhood or upbringing. Or even a past life encounter. Alternatively, an ongoing conflict with a boss or organisation forces you to take a step back. Or you're fired from a position or job. Whatever happens for you personally, it's not a time when you can forge ahead. Instead, you're wise to slow down and take your foot off the accelerator.

Your stars suggest that you'll benefit from some time out in January and February. A change of perspective could do you the world of good as 2025 gets underway.

The turning point comes on 24 February, when your ruling planet, Mars, turns direct. Then, Mars returns to Leo and your career and future sector from 18 April to 17 June. This is the time to be assertive and to push ahead with a career project or future goals.

There's a lot happening at the peak of your horoscope during the middle of the year too. The Sun is always in Leo at the height of summer in the northern hemisphere. This year, Leo season runs from 22 July to 22 August. And talk planet Mercury is in Leo for an unusually long time, from 26 June to 2 September. There seems to be a lot to negotiate, to talk about and discuss during the middle of 2025.

Like Mars at the start of the year, Mercury will be retrograde in Leo from 18 July to 11 August. Again, this is a positive period in which to slow things down. Mercury retrograde isn't the time to make a major career or future decision. Wait for Mercury to switch direction to be decisive and speak up.

As all the inner planets move through Leo this year, they will encounter your co-ruler Pluto. The key dates are 27 April, 29 June, 25 July and 27 August. This may be when you're up against opposition. Alternatively, you could be the one who decides to take a step back and prioritise family over work. Or you make a decision to retire.

There may be another personal reason why you're not as actively engaged with your future path. Perhaps you're going through a period of grief, or you have pressing priorities linked to your family, your parents or your children. Be ready to change tack when necessary and do what's right for your personal situation.

RULING PLANETS

Being a Sun Scorpio, you have two ruling planets, action planet Mars and power planet Pluto. The important planet to track is your traditional ruler Mars and where it's moving through the zodiac.

Mars rules action and get-up-and-go. It's a passionate and feisty energy, and shows you where to channel your energy and how best to crack on. As the year begins, Mars is completing its long journey through Cancer. Mars first entered Cancer on 4 September 2024, where it remained until 4 November 2024. Mars returns to Cancer in retrograde motion at the start of this year, on 6 January. Cancer is your travel and study sector. Embrace the traveller and explorer in your soul and make a pledge to educate yourself or learn a new discipline or activity. New horizons are calling.

On 18 April, Mars returns to fire sign Leo, where it turned retrograde on 6 December 2024. Leo is the star sign at the peak of your horoscope representing your career and vocation, your status and reputation. Power beckons during this transit and you're wise to rev up your ambitious nature.

On 17 June, Mars enters Virgo and your friendship and group sector. This is a positive period in the year to catch up with friends and stay connected. You might be more actively engaged with a group, club or society.

On 6 August, Mars enters Libra and the most hidden sector of your horoscope. This is a time when you're often dealing with personal issues and your attention turns inwards. Ideally, it's a time for rest and retreat. Study and research are favoured.

On 22 September, Mars enters your star sign Scorpio. This is a positive time to focus on your personal goals and aims. You have the willpower to get fit or you may feel more determined and ambitious to press ahead with your life goals.

On 4 November, Mars enters Sagittarius and your personal money sector. This is a good time to actively pursue money-making projects and put your energy and ambition into finances. Be wary of over spending or being too extravagant.

Finally, on 15 December, Mars enters earth sign Capricorn and your communication and community sector. Step into a position of authority and gain respect. Make new influential friends.

LUCKY DATES

Mars turns direct in Cancer – 24 February

Your Full Moon Scorpio – achievement/culmination – 12 May

Mars Virgo sextile Jupiter Cancer – 22 June

Mars Scorpio trine Jupiter Cancer – 28 October

Sun Scorpio trine Jupiter Cancer – 17 November

Your New Moon Scorpio – new beginnings – 20 November

Venus Scorpio trine Jupiter Cancer – 26 November

Mercury turns direct in Scorpio – 29 November

SAGITTARIUS

YOUR 2025 HOROSCOPE

SAGITTARIUS RULERSHIPS

ZODIAC SYMBOL: THE ARCHER

RULING PLANET: JUPITER,
THE PLANET OF OPPORTUNITY
AND EXPANSION

MODE/ELEMENT: MUTABLE FIRE –
ADVENTUROUS, HEDONISTIC,
BIG-PICTURE THINKING

COLOUR: PURPLE

ARCHETYPE: THE EXPLORER,
THE TRUTH-SEEKER

YOUR TOP TIPS FOR 2025

FALL IN LOVE, FIND THE
RELATIONSHIP THAT'S RIGHT FOR YOU

BOOST YOUR WEALTH, IMPROVE
YOUR FINANCIAL SECURITY

MASTER A NEW SKILL,
TURN A HOBBY INTO A JOB

PRESERVE THE MEMORIES OF YOUR PAST

TAKE AN EXTENDED HOLIDAY,
PRIORITISE YOUR WELL-BEING

LOVE AND RELATIONSHIPS

Being a Sun Sagittarius, your ruling planet is Jupiter, the biggest planet and the best planet in astrology. Therefore, you're wise to follow wherever Jupiter goes as this is where opportunity lies.

As 2025 begins, Jupiter is in your opposite star sign, Gemini, your relationship sector. Jupiter entered Gemini on 25 May 2024 where it remains until 9 June. Therefore, the first few months of 2025 are a wonderful period to get love right and do whatever it takes to bring happiness your way. While Jupiter's in Gemini, you may hear wedding bells, receive a proposal or fall head over heels in love. Jupiter expands what it touches and your personal relationships are under the cosmic spotlight.

Jupiter is the planet of liberation and freedom. Therefore, what's important is finding the relationship that's right for you and doing relationships the way you want. This may include ending a relationship or partnership that's not going well. Jupiter is about giving as well as receiving and encouraging the flow of love. Reach out to other people and create successful unions in your life.

Gemini doesn't only rule your personal relationships but all your significant one-to-ones. This includes joint ventures, your PA or personal trainer, your accountant or best friend. Jupiter's journey through Gemini is encouraging you to appreciate the people in your life. And to recognise what you give to other people as well. As Gemini is the star sign of communication, you could be working as a mediator or negotiator. Or perhaps you become a coach or counsellor.

Jupiter in Gemini teams up with planets in Aquarius and your communication sector on 30 January and 3 February. This puts you at the heart of the new air sign era, which kicks in this year. Line up an important meeting, interview or negotiation. The air signs – Gemini, Libra, Aquarius – represent communication, networks and the information highways. Air signs want to learn, gain knowledge, share and pass on ideas. You're at the heart of this information hub, with Jupiter in Gemini and power planet Pluto in Aquarius.

Pluto moved in and out of Aquarius and your communication sector in 2023/2024. This year, Pluto is established in Aquarius and will remain in this sector of your horoscope for the next twenty years. This gives your voice power and you might be stepping into a new role within society. Aquarius is the star sign of the collective and is linked to community in your horoscope. Consider where you want to make new connections and collaborations close to home. You could set up a neighbourhood watch scheme or start a community initiative that encourages people to talk. You could be actively engaged empowering people to work together as a team.

Pluto is powerful this year during Aquarius season, which runs from 19 January to 18 February. Set some New Year's resolutions linked to your voice, whether this is the year you start a podcast, write a blog or step into a role as teacher or tour guide.

Passion is on the rise too, especially once the planet of love,

Venus, enters fire sign Aries and your romance sector on 4 February. Venus in Aries loves the thrill of the chase. If you're single, make sure dating is high on your list of priorities.

Venus wants to charge ahead in Aries but slows down on 2 March when it turns retrograde. Venus's retrograde phase lasts for forty days and it's the mid-way point that's powerful. This is when the Sun and Venus come together in Aries on 23 March. It's a significant turning point and can be a time of deep insight and revelation. As this falls in your romance sector, you may be diving deep into a passionate liaison. Perhaps it's a love affair that has to remain private. Or you go back to an ex or a child-hood sweetheart reappears in your life.

Retrograde planets turn your attention inward. Venus retro-grade can be a time of learning about love and what you want when it comes to love. Use this period in the year to explore your emotional life fully.

Venus turns direct on 13 April and moves back into Aries from 30 April to 6 June. This is when you can pursue a passion wholeheartedly. Before then, there's a lovely encounter between the Sun in Aries and Jupiter in Gemini on 6 April. These two planets together promise luck and good fortune. It's exciting astrology and promising for joyful and happy relationships.

Your ruler, Jupiter, teams up with Mercury in Aries on 5 May and Venus in Aries on 5 June. Both dates are great for romance and enjoying love. Anything that begins under a Jupiter aspect promises success.

The peak date for love and relationships is arguably 8 June, when there's a Mercury–Jupiter conjunction in Gemini, your relationship sector. This is significant because Mercury is your partner planet and this would be a perfect date for a proposal or making a love agreement.

There's an educational feel about this combination too. Perhaps you enter into couples therapy or attend a course on relationships. It could play out in different ways. It's an ideal date to sign and seal a joint venture or business partnership deal. Where are you saying yes to partnership in your life?

Jupiter leaves Gemini on 9 June but that's not the end of planetary activity in your opposite star sign. Love planet Venus is in Gemini from 4 July to 31 July, a promising time for love and relationships. Then, on 7 July, live-wire Uranus moves into Gemini – a rare event, as it takes Uranus over eighty years to circuit the zodiac. Notice what occurs when Uranus changes star sign, as this is the planet of spontaneity and sudden happenings.

Uranus remains in Gemini until 8 November and will return to your relationship sector on 26 April 2026 for the following seven years. Excitement is promised on 12 August and 29 August, thanks to Uranus teaming up with planets in Aries and your romance sector. This isn't a stable influence, however – Uranus is the planet linked to splits and divorce. So there could be a revolution going on this year within your relationships. Uranus brings the unexpected and it's a catalyst for someone new coming into your life. You could enter into an unconventional relationship or be attracted to someone who's not your usual type. Anything goes with Uranus and it's a lightning bolt awakening your relationship sector.

MONEY AND COLLABORATIONS

As 2025 begins, you may not be feeling optimistic about money matters. And there are a couple of reasons for this. Firstly, action planet Mars is retrograde at the start of the year and moves back into Cancer and your joint finance sector on 6 January. Mars is on go slow until 24 February – so this is not the time to push ahead with financial ventures. If anything, you're wise to take your foot off the accelerator, so you don't make the wrong move.

Mars wants action and it can feel frustrating when you can't get ahead or things go wrong. However, you're wise to tread slowly. Plan your financial strategy and decide what needs to change to fix your personal situation moving forward.

Once Mars turns direct on 24 February, then you can start to make decisions and investments with confidence. Mars remains in Cancer until 18 April. Decisions made at the start of the year may be what enables your finances to grow and flourish, once Jupiter moves into this sector of your horoscope later in the year.

In addition, you no longer have Pluto in Capricorn, your personal money sector. Pluto entered Capricorn in 2008. Then, in 2023/2024, Pluto started its journey out of your money sector. Pluto is an extreme planet. Therefore, you may have experienced debt or bankruptcy while Pluto was in Capricorn. Or perhaps it went the other way and you became a billionaire or 'pluto-crat'. It's not an easy influence, however, as Pluto adds intensity and obsession to the mix. As 2025 is the first year that you no longer have Pluto in your money sector, it's an ideal time to shift your attitude, do things differently and boost your wealth.

Jupiter leaves behind air sign Gemini on 9 June and enters water sign Cancer, where it remains until 30 June 2026. Your planet Jupiter's journey through Cancer is when finances can grow and flourish.

Even though Jupiter is leaving your relationship sector, the focus remains on other people and joint ventures. In particular, shared finances and resources, as this is one of the money sectors of your horoscope. When it comes to relationships, this is the planetary equivalent of the settling-down period – creating a joint bank account and learning to share your life with another person. Cancer rules sex and intimacy in your horoscope too, so turn your attention to your desires and seeking emotional fulfilment or satisfaction.

When Jupiter is in Cancer, it's the perfect time to get expert advice, especially when it comes to finance or legal matters. Jupiter is a global planet so there are no restrictions and you can expand your circle of expertise.

Jupiter in Cancer can be an abundant force in your life, when you receive an inheritance, a gift or bonus. It's a significant time to focus on your future security and create strong financial foundations for yourself and the ones you love.

There are two stand-out dates when Jupiter's in Cancer: 24 June and 12 August. This is when there's a Sun–Jupiter conjunction followed by a Venus–Jupiter conjunction. Both these aspects are promising for wealth and financial moves. Perhaps you receive financial help and support. Or you're the one who steps in to gift others. These would be promising dates for investments and improving your financial prospects.

As a Sun Sagittarius, you're a natural entrepreneur and this has a lot to do with your ruling planet, Jupiter. Jupiter is a reminder that luck is an attitude. When you have a big vision, a willingness to take risks and you have belief in yourself and what you're doing, you attract good fortune into your life.

Use Jupiter's journey through Cancer and your finance sector to improve your fortunes. Cancer is a caring and protective star sign linked to home and family. Therefore, you might be considering a property deal or be keen to combine your resources with family or loved ones, to take care of one another. While Jupiter's moving through Cancer, you might want to ask for a pay rise or go for promotion: 22 June, 12 September and 8 October are promising dates for both, as Jupiter connects with the inner planets in Virgo and your career and vocation sector.

Jupiter is lively towards the end of the year too, when it teams up with planets in Scorpio on 24 October, 28 October, 17 November, 22 November, 26 November and 6 December. Scorpio is the star sign before yours and this is a karmic influence. You may be repaid for your kindnesses in the past. Or perhaps you benefit from your past, through a benefactor. Alternatively, you may be involved in fundraising or a charity venture.

The only proviso is that Mercury is retrograde from 9 November to 29 November. When the planet of communication is moving backward through the zodiac, it can be a topsy-turvy time for the money markets. That doesn't mean you can't take advantage of what's happening. Do your research, rework your financial strategy and read between the lines. Once Mercury turns direct on 29 November, put your plans and ideas into action.

As Jupiter moves through your finance sector in the second half of the year, it grows stronger when it aligns with other planets. This means that you're likely to do better financially when you team up with other people and get the right experts and advisers on your side.

CREATIVITY AND COMMITMENT

Saturn is the slowest moving of the traditional planets and spends two-to-three years in one star sign. This year, Saturn changes star sign on 25 May when it enters Aries. Saturn remains in Aries until 1 September but will return to this sector of your horoscope from 14 February 2026 to April 2028. Aries is a fellow fire sign and linked to fun and play in your horoscope. It represents the things in life you 'give birth to', including children, creative projects, and your gifts, skills and talents.

Having Saturn entering the sector of your horoscope which rules creativity and self-expression may not feel easy at first. This is because Saturn can be a gloomy influence and it's the planet linked to work rather than play. However, what this is helpful for is committing to a daily practice and being self-disciplined. If there's something you want to master, an instrument, art or craft, tap into Saturn's persistent nature in your creativity sector. It may take you hours of commitment, but Saturn can help you get the job done.

With Saturn in Aries, you might be using your skills and talents in your work and combining the two. As a fire sign, you tend to have high levels of motivation and your energy and enthusiasm means you're good at starting things. However, you're not always as disciplined at seeing things through to completion. This may change with Saturn in Aries.

There is a cautionary note, though, and this is not to squeeze the joy out of an activity because you're being overly critical of yourself or you're trying too hard. Your enthusiasm may wane quickly if a passion becomes a chore, even if it involves an activity you enjoy. Saturn can be a harsh taskmaster and it's advisable to balance the more serious side of this planet with a light and joyful attitude. This applies to parenting too, as Aries rules children and pregnancy in your horoscope. Saturn can be a strict influence, so notice when you take this too far. Find a comfortable balance when it comes to setting boundaries.

Make a conscious effort to have fun with your kids and remember to encourage and give praise where it's due.

Set up some new commitments that not only fulfil you on a deep level but bring stability and regular support to other people in your life. If you've been thinking about starting a family, adopting a pet or becoming a mentor to teenagers, Saturn's move into Aries is the ideal time to make that commitment.

Saturn isn't moving into Aries on its own this year, as there's another major planet changing star sign. This is one of the generational planets, Neptune, which enters Aries on 30 March, where it stays until 22 October. Like Saturn, Neptune will return to Aries next year on 26 January 2026 and remain in Aries for the following seven years. Neptune is the opposite influence to Saturn. While Saturn represents reality and hard work, Neptune is the planet of dreams and the imagination. Working together, these planetary archetypes can be helpful in turning your dreams into reality.

In June, July and August, the two planets are side by side. This is in preparation for their epic conjunction in February 2026, which is the first time these two planets will meet since 1989. This combination could work well for you, as it's compassionate and idealistic, but also real and enterprising. This could be the year you turn a hobby into a job or you get involved with an organisation that benefits children's mental health and well-being. Stand-out dates when Saturn and Neptune team up with Uranus in Gemini, your partnership sector, may be 12 August and 29 August. This could symbolise meeting the person who's willing to parent with you or finding the right partner or teacher to pursue your creative goals.

In 2023 and 2024, there were two New Moon solar eclipses

in Aries and this same sector of your horoscope. This year, on 29 March, there's a third and final solar eclipse in Aries. Solar eclipses are turbo-powered New Moons, urging you to leap into action and start something new. They add courage and boldness to the mix, and accelerate growth. Therefore, things may have been moving at top speed in your life, whether linked to children, creativity, romance or love affairs.

However, the eclipse in March falls during a double retrograde phase. The planet of love and relating, Venus, is retrograde from 2 March to 13 April and talk planet Mercury is retrograde from 15 March to 7 April. This means that something may be seeded in your life during the solar eclipse but that you may have to be patient for things to flourish and grow. Also, take note of Saturn's move into Aries urging you to be more persistent and patient and not to give up.

There is a proviso not to throw your money around during the retrograde phases. They aren't the time to make a major decision or investment. Also, the period from 15 June to 19 June is a red flag for spending money. Be wary about making a gesture of generosity to a child or lover and rein in being overly extravagant. This might be funding a hobby or leisure activity. That's not to say you can't enjoy yourself. Yet your stars are encouraging you to be more discerning about where you invest your time, energy and money.

Whether you're diving deep into love, starting a family or enjoying a season of festivals and fire sign fun, it's important that you find an outlet for your passion.

HOME AND FAMILY

Since March 2023, Saturn has been in Pisces, the star sign at the base of your horoscope. Pisces rules your home and family, your legacy and roots, your past and where you come from. Saturn's influence can be challenging at the base of your horoscope. You may have been trapped by family commitments or burdened by a home or property situation.

The other planet that's been in Pisces since 2012 is romantic Neptune. Perhaps you've been living on a boat or you bought property close to a lake, river or the sea.

This year, Saturn and Neptune are changing star sign and begin to complete their journeys through your home and family sector. Saturn moves out of Pisces from 25 May to 1 September, while Neptune exits Pisces from 30 March to 22 October. Therefore, you would expect some major shifts taking place around home and family. Saturn's move out of Pisces could feel like a burden lifting. You may sense you have more options moving forward and no longer feel tied to the past.

Saturn is the planet of duty and commitment. Therefore, looking after your family, your parents or running a home or property may have become a major priority in your life.

Pisces' energy peaks in the first few months of this year, before Saturn and Neptune move on, and it's likely to be emotional. At times, you may experience a sense of overwhelm or feel confused about where you're heading and why as there's so much happening. The social planets Mercury and Venus spend an unusually long time in Pisces. Mercury is here from 14 February to 3 March and again from 30 March to 16 April. Venus is in Pisces from 3 January to 4 February, and again from 27 March to 30 April. You may be involved in property negotiations, or perhaps you've got the builders or decorators in. There may be a lot to talk about and discuss as you prepare for a big family celebration. This could be a wedding, anniversary or a holiday gathering the clans.

Both Venus and Mercury are retrograde during March and April. This favours going on retreat or taking a trip down memory lane. Retrograde planets turn your attention to what's behind you. Pisces is an empathic star sign, emotional and sensitive. It's linked to images, dreams and sentimentality. You could be exploring your family tree, be preserving photographs or caring for family heirlooms. One way or another, you're immersed in the past.

There's another significant planetary factor taking place on 12 January, when the North Node enters Pisces, where it will remain until 26 July 2026. The nodes are closely connected to the path of destiny and the wheel of fortune turning. This suggests that your family will be your greatest learning and you may be acutely aware of the ties that bind you. Destiny may step in this year to move you in a new direction.

The nodes are also connected to the eclipses and, this year, the major eclipse cycle cuts across the Virgo/Pisces axis of the zodiac. This represents the foundations of your life and the link between your past and your future. This eclipse cycle started in September 2024 and will complete in February 2027. The eclipse cycles repeat every 18–19 years and this may be significant for you regarding what's happening this year. Your career and your future path, your home and family, your past and where you come from are where major changes are likely to be taking place.

This year, there are two Full Moon lunar eclipses cutting across the Virgo/Pisces axis of the zodiac on 14 March and 7

September. Eclipses bring what's hidden to light and Full Moons tend to be emotional and dramatic. Whatever's revealed on or around the eclipses, you're wise not to act immediately. Allow your emotions to settle and wait a while before taking action. Perhaps you're juggling the work/life balance and changes at work or within your family necessitate a new way of doing things.

You could spend a lot of time daydreaming about the past or be pulled back into the past because of what's happening in the present day and your current situation. Yet you recognise where you need to let go and surrender and put your trust and faith in life.

Honour the loving connections in your life but take a symbolic step forward that moves you into the future. Don't let guilt or fear consume you and don't remain beholden to the past if it no longer serves you.

WORK AND CAREER

The earth signs represent work and money in your horoscope. Earth signs don't have the same dynamic spark that fire signs do, your element. Instead, they prove that when you're reliable, steady and hard-working, you reap your rewards.

However, there is one planetary influence in your horoscope that is bringing something different and unique to your working life: the planet of unconventionality, Uranus, which has been moving through Taurus and your work and lifestyle sector since 2018. Uranus in Taurus favours freelance work, which suits your Sagittarius nature. If you're typical of your Sun sign, you may be an entrepreneur or run an online business that you can do from anywhere – 'have laptop, will travel'. You often don't fit easily into a conventional work situation, as you like your freedom and you prefer to do things your way. Uranus in Taurus encourages you to work smart not hard.

This year, Uranus is moving on. Uranus leaves Taurus on 7 July and will return on 8 November until 26 April 2026, so your situation is shifting and can't remain the same. If you want to apply for a job, take a business online or start something new and different, leap in when Uranus is active. The key dates are 17 May, 24 May and 4 July, when Uranus is in action at the same time as the inner planets are moving through Taurus. Uranus favours impulsive moves, which suits your fire sign nature.

This year, Uranus in Taurus makes two major planetary aspects – connections formed between planets – to Saturn and Neptune in Pisces, your home and family sector. These take place on 4 April and 20 November. This might be the year that you set up a business working from home, if you haven't already. Or you team up with a family member to start a new part-time job.

Also, note what happens later in the year when there are not one but two New Moons taking place in Virgo and your career and vocation sector. The first New Moon falls on 23 August, a symbol of new beginnings. New Moons are great for launching a new project or starting over. Be proactive and say yes to a new opportunity. Keep your gaze on your future path and fire some arrows high into the sky to see where they land.

The second New Moon is a solar eclipse in Virgo, which falls on 21 September, the day before the equinox. A solar eclipse is a turbo-powered New Moon packed full with potential. Sometimes, a solar eclipse is the portal to a new era, a new chapter in your life. However, one door may close before a new door opens. There's often a theme of endings and beginnings when a solar eclipse kicks in.

If you don't have the freedom or independence you crave on a daily basis, the solar eclipse could inspire you. You may feel ready to take a leap of faith and set your life up in a way that suits you. You do, however, have to be careful and check your motives before you cut and run. If you're making your life less stressful by moving on, good news. Yet if you haven't got a clue what's next, this may well add stress to your life, so proceed cautiously.

The trickiest period in the year may be the last couple of months when Uranus is back in Taurus and making some challenging oppositions. The key dates are 19 November, 21 November, 30 November and 10 December. This could be a period in the year when you notice your stress levels rising. You might feel distracted or out of sorts – particularly if, for example, a freelance lifestyle isn't giving you the security you need.

Uranus can be an erratic and unpredictable influence. You may find it challenging if you're being pulled in too many different directions or spending too much time on technology. Bear in mind that Taurus rules your health and well-being as well as your work and lifestyle. Even though freedom may be a goal, there may be times when your current job or lifestyle works against you.

Uranus isn't always a calming influence. Don't lose sight of what's important to you and where your values lie as Uranus moves in and out of your work and health sector this year.

TIME OUT

Retrograde planets teach you that flow is imperative to good health. There are times to put your foot on the accelerator of life and other times when you're wise to put on the brake and stop. This year, talk planet Mercury turns retrograde in all three fire signs – Aries, Leo and Sagittarius. Mercury retrograde is an ideal time to stop and rest, retreat and recharge your batteries. This is especially important when Mercury switches direction in the element fire, your element. To avoid burnout, slow down.

Mercury's first retrograde phase, 15 March to 7 April, would suit a staycation or visiting family for some rest and relaxation. Mercury's second retrograde phase falls in the middle of the year. This is an important one to note as Mercury will be in Leo and your travel sector for an unusually long time, from 26 June to 2 September. If you're a typical Sagittarius, travel and holidays are a key feature of your life. You love exploring the world and using travel to change your perspective. This would be a wonderful year to have an extended holiday in July and August while Mercury's in Leo. If that's not possible, prioritise the Mercury retrograde phase, from 18 July to 11 August.

The final Mercury retrograde phase takes place in Sagittarius from 9 November to 29 November. This is when Mercury moves out of your star sign and back into Scorpio, the star sign before Sagittarius and the most hidden sector of your horoscope – planets here often favour inner work or spiritual growth, so this is a double whammy of introspection or quiet time.

Once action planet Mars moves into Scorpio on 22 September, this area of your horoscope is under the cosmic spotlight until mid-December. Scorpio is a healing star sign and this is a period in the year to focus on the mind-body-spirit connection. Ensure you're taking care of each part of the whole. You could dive deep into a healing therapy, go on retreat or take part in an extreme challenge. Scorpio is linked to detoxing and letting go of toxins.

It's worth diving in deep because come your birthday month, you have Mars, Venus, Mercury and the Sun all moving through your star sign Sagittarius. This can give you a confidence boost but it's important to know when to stop and recharge your energy levels leading up to this period in the year.

RULING PLANET

Your ruling planet is Jupiter, the best planet in astrology. In mythology, Jupiter was god of the sky. Jupiter's attributes are opportunity, expansion and growth, and it's the planet linked to luck and good fortune. Jupiter conjunctions are considered lucky dates and they're in the section below, also in your horoscope. This year, Jupiter's making a lot of positive planetary aspects. Track them, use them and increase Jupiter's positive influence in your life. Also, consider when your ruling planet turns direct and retrograde.

Here's the pattern: Jupiter turns direct in Gemini on 4 February; Jupiter turns retrograde in Cancer on 11 November. A planet's energy is more intense when it switches direction. This means that Jupiter is direct for most of 2025, which is good news for you. Make the most of this and grasp new opportunities when they come your way.

Finally, the date when Jupiter changes star sign, 9 June, is worth taking note of. You have all the key information explaining what it means for you in the sections above.

LUCKY DATES

Jupiter turns direct – 4 February

Sun Aries sextile Jupiter Gemini – 6 April

Venus Aries sextile Jupiter Gemini – 5 June

Mercury conjunct Jupiter Gemini – 8 June

Your Full Moon Sagittarius – achievement/culmination – 11 June

Sun conjunct Jupiter Cancer – 24 June

Venus conjunct Jupiter Cancer – 12 August

Your New Moon Sagittarius – new beginnings – 20 December

CAPRICORN

YOUR 2025 HOROSCOPE

CAPRICORN RULERSHIPS

ZODIAC SYMBOL: THE MOUNTAIN GOAT

RULING PLANET: SATURN, PLANET OF
AUTHORITY, OLD FATHER TIME

MODE/ELEMENT: CARDINAL EARTH –
HARD-WORKING, COMMITTED, RELIABLE,
RESPONSIBLE

COLOUR: DARK COLOURS –
BLACK/GREY/BROWN

ARCHETYPE: THE WORKAHOLIC,
THE HERMIT

YOUR TOP TIPS FOR 2025

AIM FOR A HEALTHY
WORK/LIFE BALANCE

PLAN A WEDDING,
FALL DEEPLY IN LOVE

BUILD YOUR DREAM HOME,
PROTECT YOUR LOVED ONES

OPEN YOUR HEART TO YOUR COMMUNITY,
BE A GOOD SAMARITAN

TRANSFORM YOUR FINANCES,
STEP INTO YOUR MONEY POWER

♑

WORK AND HEALTH

Jupiter is the biggest and best planet, representing luck and opportunity. Therefore, wherever Jupiter goes, you're wise to follow. Jupiter takes approximately one year to journey through each star sign. As the year begins, Jupiter's in Gemini and one of the practical sectors of your horoscope. This highlights your work and routine, service to others and your lifestyle and health. Jupiter entered Gemini on 25 May 2024, where it will remain until 9 June. This is a lively combination which could give you extra get-up-and-go and increase your energy levels.

While Jupiter moves through Gemini, you may find the ideal job that frees up your time. Or you fall in love with volunteering. Gemini favours multi-tasking and adding a new string to your bow. It's an ideal time to learn something new, a language or skill. It would be a good time to take part in activities and develop daily habits which boost your health and well-being. Gemini is a social air sign so don't go it alone when it comes to these key areas of your life. For example, find a gym buddy to keep you on track with your fitness goals. Or work alongside a coaching group that focuses on daily gratitude or health. If you're looking for a job, ask around.

This isn't about overnight change. It's about adjusting your routine and lifestyle on a daily basis. It's the little changes that can make the biggest difference over time. You could aim for a more balanced diet or practise intermittent fasting, whatever works for you. Gemini is linked to the spoken word so why not start or end your day listing three things you're grateful for.

Jupiter in Gemini is a reminder of the importance of connecting with people and being of service to others. You might step into a supportive role within your community, a regular practice or activity, that makes a difference to people's lives. It could be litter picking, driving the elderly to hospital or being a friend to refugees. Whatever speaks to you personally, find your place within society and do your bit to help.

Gemini season is when you may notice the difference that a new health routine or lifestyle change is making. The Sun's move through Gemini takes place this year from 20 May to 21 June, and talk planet Mercury is here from 26 May to 8 June. The Gemini influence peaks on 8 June when there's a Mercury–Jupiter conjunction in this sign. Both planets are linked to education and learning, so you might sign up for a course or win an award for your work. This combination can be a symbol of good news or hearing of an opportunity that's right up your street.

Jupiter leaves Gemini in June but another major planet moves into Gemini the following month. That planet is innovative Uranus, linked to technology and all things modern. Uranus will be in Gemini from 7 July to 8 November. Uranus returns to Gemini on 26 April 2026 and will be in this sector of your horoscope for the following seven years. Uranus is the innovator and awakener, the planet of change. This doesn't necessarily make for a steady and stable routine. In fact, you may actively want to bring about change, whether you're taking a business online or you're bored in your current position or role. Uranus likes to disrupt the status quo and you may be on a mission to revolutionise your place of work. Uranus is also linked to society and the community, so take your radical ideas out into your neighbourhood.

As Uranus moves through Gemini, it teams up with key planets in Aries and your home and family sector on 12 August and 29 August. These combinations suggest working from home or finding a job that gives you more flexibility. Perhaps you're having to juggle home and work more than usual moving forward. The reasons for this may kick in on 6 April, 5 May and 5 June, when the inner planets are moving through Aries and align with Jupiter in Gemini, bringing about an alliance between these two sectors of your horoscope. Perhaps someone in your family starts working for you during this period in the year or you decide to get fit and lead a healthier lifestyle together as a family. This symbolism can play out in different ways, so see what it means for you. The main message is to be open to new ideas, both at work and regarding your health. Recognise the joy of improving your everyday routine and take care of the mind-body-spirit connection.

Do what's necessary to boost your energy levels and appreciate all that life has to offer. Play your cards right and your work, health and routine could be zinging with life and vitality.

LOVE AND RELATIONSHIPS

The planet of opportunity, Jupiter, enters your opposite star sign, Cancer, your relationship sector, on 9 June, where it will remain until 30 June 2026. This could be a wonderful period to get love right and do whatever you need to bring happiness your way.

As a Capricorn, the planet that rules partnership in your horoscope is the Moon. The Moon is the ruler of your opposite star sign, Cancer, a nurturing and comforting influence. Therefore, you may be attracted to a partner who represents the qualities of the Moon, with kindness and loyalty at the top of your wish list. Ensure that your relationships are affectionate and loving moving forward.

While Jupiter's moving through your relationship sector, there may be wedding bells. Or you and your partner decide to renew your vows.

Jupiter is about giving as well as receiving. Therefore, the more you open your heart, the more you allow love in. If you're a typical Capricorn, you can have a reserved side to your nature. This isn't the year to hold back when it comes to love. Jupiter in Cancer is encouraging you to live life from the heart and fully embrace your close relationships. Take joy from all your relationships and be around people who are loving and kind and lift your spirits.

This year, Jupiter's influence in Cancer peaks on 24 June and 12 August, when there's a Sun–Jupiter conjunction followed by a Venus–Jupiter conjunction in Cancer. If you're in a relationship or married, plan something special with your other half. Perhaps, you choose these dates to celebrate love. The love planet Venus will be moving through Cancer and your relationship sector from 31 July to 25 August. There could be good news for your other half, giving you both reason to celebrate. Jupiter's themes of opportunity, expansion and good fortune are blessing your partnerships.

Love and travel are linked this year, when the inner planets move through your travel sector, Virgo, and align with Jupiter in Cancer. The key dates are 22 June, 12 September and 8 October. If you're looking for a holiday romance, head off on your travels while love planet Venus is in Virgo from 19 September to 13 October. This would be a gorgeous month for a second honeymoon or romantic holiday.

Later in the year, Jupiter teams up with the inner planets in Scorpio and your friendship sector. The key dates are 24 October, 28 October, 17 November, 26 November and 6 December. These combinations link love and friendship. If you're a typical Capricorn, you often have loyal friends in your life who you've known since childhood. This year, friendship could develop into love and Scorpio is the star sign linked to sexuality and intimacy. If you're in a relationship or married, actively engage with your social life together as a couple.

Don't rush into anything from 9 November to 29 November, however, when Mercury's retrograde. Yet, do favour intimacy, heart to hearts and soul-mate connections.

Jupiter rules freedom too and, in Cancer, this could be the catalyst you need to break free from a difficult or controlling relationship. Jupiter brings joy and it's about creating the relationship situation that's right for you. Jupiter in Cancer could spell good news for a business partnership or any one-to-one collaboration.

The trickiest period for relationships while Jupiter's in Cancer may be 15 June to 19 June. This is when Jupiter clashes with your ruling planet, Saturn, and Neptune in Aries and your home and family sector. Perhaps there's an issue with your in-laws. Or there are limits or obstacles linked to home or family, which make it challenging for love to flourish.

Also, as the year begins, you may not be feeling the love.

This is because passion planet Mars is retrograde as 2025 gets underway. Mars moves back through Cancer and your relationship sector from 6 January to 24 February. This suggests that relationships may be on the back foot as the year begins. Sometimes when Mars is in retreat, you go back to an ex or revisit your romantic past. Or your libido's low and you're feeling frustrated about love. Mars rules anger as well as passion. Therefore, the best way to use Mars in your relationship sector is to confront any issues, be assertive and clear the air. Take decisive action after 24 February when Mars is back to direct motion and in your relationship sector until 18 April.

There is another significant factor linked to love in your horoscope. Since 2018, the planet Uranus has been in Taurus and the sector of your horoscope which rules romance and love affairs. This rarely makes for a steady and stable love life. Instead, it can indicate unexpected events and stop-start love affairs.

Sometimes, you notice the effect of a planet more when it changes star sign. As Uranus remains in one star sign for approximately seven years, this doesn't happen often. This year, Uranus is beginning to move away from Taurus and will be gone completely in April 2026. Uranus is in Taurus up until 7 July and from 8 November onwards. It is active during Taurus season, which runs from 19 April to 20 May, plus there are some lively Uranus conjunctions on 17 May, 24 May and again on 4 July.

If you're in a relationship or married, anything goes, especially regarding children and pregnancy, as Taurus rules this sector of your horoscope. There could be news of a birth or an unexpected pregnancy. If you're trying to get pregnant, be spontaneous and make love when the fancy takes you. If you're looking for love, be daring and make the first move. This may feel like venturing into the unknown, which doesn't always suit your Capricorn nature. Yet sometimes a risk is worth taking and Uranus encourages impulsive behaviour. Do what feels right in the moment. This may include choosing to be single or playing the field.

Your stars in 2025 are encouraging you to deepen your close relationships and be more adventurous when it comes to love.

HOME AND FAMILY

Your ruling planet is Saturn, the planet of authority, linked to tradition and history. Saturn takes almost thirty years to circuit the zodiac and is an important planet for you to track. This year, Saturn changes star sign, entering Aries – your home and family sector – on 25 May, where it remains until 1 September. It's back in Aries next year, on 14 February 2026 until April 2028.

Aries is the star sign at the base of your horoscope. It's about your past, your legacy and where you come from. Saturn in your home and family sector can be a grounding and rooted influence. You may put family first for a specific reason. Or perhaps you're caring for someone close. Saturn is the planet of commitment and, wherever Saturn goes, duty and responsibility follow. Traditionally, it's not a time to move home when Saturn is in this sector of your horoscope. Instead, focus on putting down roots where you are.

You may be establishing yourself somewhere new. Or perhaps you're applying for residency or building your own home. Saturn represents rules and regulations, forms and bureaucracy. Sometimes, Saturn stops you in your tracks and you're faced with limitation or obstacles. Try not to become too rigid or inflexible if you run into a dead end. Be purposeful but be wary of sticking too closely to the rules, as this could limit your options.

Saturn's move into Aries comes after a significant eclipse cycle that's been cutting across the Aries/Libra axis of the zodiac. This represents the foundations of your life, your past and your future path. Aries rules your home and family and Libra rules your career and status. This eclipse cycle started in April 2023 and completes in March this year. This is often a time when you change job or move home. Sometimes the two are linked – i.e. you have to move to follow work, or changes at home and within your family necessitate a rethink about your next steps.

This year, there's a powerful New Moon solar eclipse in Aries on 29 March. This follows on from solar eclipses at the base of your horoscope in 2023 and 2024. Solar Eclipses are power points of energy and accelerate growth when you can move things forward and fast. However, any new beginning often stems from an ending – i.e. one door has to close before a new door opens.

Consider what you're trying to push through or initiate close to the eclipse. This might be linked to a property deal or taking charge of a family situation. You could step in as guardian to a child or be asked to take responsibility for a member of your family.

However, there are two planets retrograde while this eclipse takes place. When planets are retrograde, this isn't the best time to make a decision or an investment. Talk planet Mercury is retrograde from 15 March to 7 April and the planet of love and money, Venus, is retrograde from 2 March to 13 April. During this double retrograde phase, you may be playing a waiting game. Retrograde planets turn your attention inwards and it's a time for reflection rather than action. Alternatively, you might be on a staycation or be taking a trip down memory lane. Look at what may be coming to an end during this phase too or where you need to do things differently. There could be a specific reason why you have to drop everything to be there for someone close. Or you may be considering starting a family or moving closer to family. You may spend an unusually long time with members of your family this year. Or perhaps you're involved in a major renovation or DIY project. The turning point comes mid-April when you can start to move things forward and respond to what's been happening.

Another major planet is influencing your home and family sector and that planet is Neptune. Neptune is one of the slower-moving generational planets and is currently moving closer to your ruling planet, Saturn. Neptune enters Aries on 30 March where it remains until 22 October. Neptune will return to Aries on 26 January 2026 and be in your home and family sector until 2038/2039. Neptune is the planet of sentimentality and this may pull you back into the past. Perhaps, you're drawing up your family tree or you're sorting out old photographs and handling family heirlooms.

Saturn and Neptune are side by side in June, July and August preparing for their epic conjunction in Aries in February 2026. This is the first time these two planets will come together since 1989. They are unusual bedfellows as Saturn rules reality and Neptune rules fantasy. Saturn represents boundaries, whereas Neptune is boundless. Yet both planets honour the past and together, they want to be keepers of the past. Ideally, harness the energies of both planets and have them working together. For example, this combination could see you turning your dream home into reality. Or you set up a refuge for vulnerable people or start an antiques business.

What you need to be wary of is allowing any guilt from your past to pervade into the present day. If there are wounds to heal, make this a priority. Be wary of falling into fear or doubt or being paranoid about keeping your home and family safe. Your home may be your castle but don't let it become your prison. Ultimately, remember that home is where the heart is.

COMMUNICATION AND COMMUNITY

Saturn and Neptune are moving in and out of star sign Pisces this year. Saturn is in Pisces up until 25 May and again from 1 September, while Neptune is in Pisces up until 30 March and again from 22 October. Both planets are starting to complete their journeys through this sector of your horoscope.

Pisces is your communication sector, ruling the spoken and written word, linked to study and teaching. Your planet, Saturn, entered Pisces in March 2023 and will depart Pisces for the next thirty years in February 2026.

As Saturn rules commitment and discipline, you may be engaged with a comprehensive course of study, or you're stepping into a role as teacher and passing on your wisdom. Saturn in Pisces is helpful for writing and creative projects, as Saturn is the planet of self-discipline. Alternatively, you could become a voice of authority and step into a significant role within your community. Pisces rules your local neighbourhood, making new friends, your siblings and close relatives.

There's an inclusive feel to Saturn and Neptune in Pisces. And, during the first few months of 2025, there's a flood of activity in this sector of your horoscope. This is about sharing emotional connections with other people and using your emotions to transform society. Lead with the heart and consider where you might be able to step in and help or support others. Where in your life can you work alongside other people to create a wave of compassionate energy?

Both the planet of communication, Mercury, and the planet of relating, Venus, spend an unusually long time in Pisces early in the year. Venus is in Pisces from 3 January to 4 February and again from 27 March to 30 April. Mercury is in Pisces from 14 February to 3 March, and again from 30 March to 16 April. What this means is that there's a flow of activity in this sector and, as Mercury and Venus move back and forth, they interact with Saturn, Neptune and the North Node in Pisces numerous times. It's a flood of emotional connection and you can't help but be pulled along with it.

Perhaps you become a student of spirituality or you're working on a film. You may be writing poetry avidly or be composing music. Or you meet up with a group locally that helps you to feel loved and connected. Step into something new and extraordinary. Though this could be as simple as a weekly conversation with a sibling or neighbour which deepens your relationship.

Pisces is a caring water sign and Saturn in Pisces is less interested in playing by the rules. What this represents for you may become clear when Saturn and Neptune team up with innovative Uranus in Taurus on 4 April and 30 November. Consider what new role you're stepping into, whether in the shape of parenting, partnering or leading the way.

This may be linked to a deeper calling. This is because on 12 January, the North Node enters Pisces where it remains until

26 July 2026. So listen to your inner voice early in the year and be guided by your emotions. The nodes often coincide with signs and synchronicities appearing in your life. This process is helped when you start tapping into your intuition.

If you're a typical Capricorn, you tend to be practical and like to deal with the reality of a situation. Yet, there's a lot that can be learned by following an alternative path, one that encourages you to surrender to life. Aim to be in flow with the universe and follow your inner knowingness.

There's another reason why you're entering a new phase in 2025 and this involves the current eclipse cycle. This cuts across the Virgo/Pisces axis of the zodiac, which rules education in your horoscope, also encompassing study, teaching, philosophy and religion. It's about how you engage with the world and other people, and how you make the most of your learning opportunities.

There are two powerful Full Moon lunar eclipses here, one in Virgo on 14 March and one in Pisces on 7 September. Sometimes, eclipses coincide with drama and they can be important turning points. What happens close to the eclipse date could impact you emotionally and be a catalyst for change. You might be affected by what's going on in the world or you undergo a spiritual awakening or have a profound religious experience.

However this plays out for you, know that you're being pulled in a new direction. This is likely to be less about work, money and status, and more about where you find meaning and purpose in life. It's what takes you beyond the mundane and everyday, and connects you with life and the universe on a deeper level.

If there's something you believe in or you want to communicate to others, don't hold back. You might be speaking up for your community, experimenting with a New Age activity or engaging with an alternative group of people. Find your voice and find your place within society.

MONEY AND FUTURE PATH

If you're a typical Capricorn, you like to have a mountain to climb, whether literally or metaphorically. You get things done when you have a plan and long-term goals. Your star sign is notoriously ambitious and there's a side to your nature that wants to achieve and be successful, favouring status and reputation. However, there may be times in your life when this doesn't ring true for you and you sense something new growing and developing within you. Your values emerge from a deeper, more spiritual place.

This year, you could sense a shift happening. This has a lot to do with the fact that an important eclipse cycle is coming to a close. This is the Aries/Libra eclipse cycle which began in March 2023 and completes in March this year. This is often a significant period of change, as Aries and Libra are the star signs which cut across the foundations of your horoscope. It's the connection between the past and your future and where you juggle home and work. Libra rules your career and vocation, your status and reputation, your future and where you're heading. Aries rules your home and family, your past and where you come from.

During this eclipse cycle, which takes place every 18–19 years, there's often a change to your career or vocational path. Eclipses are about the wheel of fortune turning, accelerating growth. Sometimes, the unexpected happens to speed up the process of change. Although as this eclipse cycle completes this year, you may start to settle into a new chapter or phase.

Also this year, there's significant planetary activity in your money sectors. Firstly, power planet Pluto is now established in Aquarius, your personal money sector, where it will remain for the next twenty years. Pluto has been moving in and out of your star sign, Capricorn, and your money sector, Aquarius, throughout 2023/2024, bringing something new to this area of your life. Perhaps, you sold a business or made some savvy investments in the last couple of years and your financial fortunes are on the up. Alternatively, Pluto moving in and out of Aquarius may have coincided with a period of loss. At its most extreme, Pluto in Aquarius can symbolise bankruptcy or debt.

Pluto is the power planet and you may already know a lot about its pull as it's been moving through Capricorn since 2008. You may already have had a personal encounter with Pluto. This planet works in your favour when you have laser focus and you use your power to good effect. You may recognise the power of money, while Pluto's in Aquarius. There's a theme of regeneration or passing on the legacy of money.

This year, Pluto is powerful during Aquarius season from 19 January to 18 February. The period from 21 January to 3 February could be exceptional. This might be linked to your job or perhaps your health. It could symbolise a pay-out or a pay-rise.

Since the middle of 2023, all the inner planets have spent some time retrograde in Leo. This flags up a stop-start scenario to money matters, as along with Aquarius, Leo also rules finances in your horoscope. As 2025 begins, action planet Mars is retrograde here, having turned retrograde in Leo on 6 December 2024.

What's significant this year is that the planets moving through Leo will all be opposed by Pluto in Aquarius – the key dates are 3 January, 27 April, 29 June, 25 July and 27 August. You may have to be ruthless on or around these dates, especially if other people are trying to get their hands on your money. This could be the government, an ex or a third party.

The time to be assertive when it comes to finances is when Mars gets back up to speed in Leo from 18 April to 17 June. Life is calling you to bring your courage and determination to your finances. Set new systems in place that work for you, find the right financial associations, advisers and experts, and stand strong.

Also this year, communication planet, Mercury, will be in Leo and your joint finance sector for an unusually long time – from 26 June to 2 September – and will be retrograde in Leo from 18 July to 11 August. As Mercury is linked to the money markets, this is often a time when the financial world is topsy-turvy. On a personal level, you're wise not to make any major investments or financial deals while Mercury's retrograde. Instead, plan your strategy, do your research and get ready to act once Mercury is back to direct motion mid-August.

Pluto will come into its own in Aquarius over the next few years. For now, you're wise to work with this new influence in your horoscope. Aquarius rules money, assets and possessions, also your values and self-worth. Change your money mindset and adopt a wealthy attitude. Be determined to transform any beliefs that might hold you back. The power behind money lies in your personal growth and enterprises, rather than relying too heavily on other people for your future financial success.

EARTH SIGN PLEASURE

If you're looking for pleasure, look to the earth signs in your horoscope, Capricorn, Taurus and Virgo. The earth signs relate to your personal fulfilment, the things in life you love: play, fun and adventure.

Capricorn season, your birthday month – 21 December to 19 January – starts and ends the year. This is a cosmic reminder to set your resolutions as one year begins and rest well as another year ends. Be in flow with nature and take your foot off the accelerator of life when it's your birthday season.

Taurus is the star sign that represents creativity, fun, entertainment and pleasure. Innovative Uranus is here until 7 July and again from 3 November. This is encouraging you to be spontaneous, say yes to life and ensure fun and games are high priority. If you're a typical Capricorn, you like to plan ahead, but use Uranus's influence in your fun sector to practise leaping in and being impulsive. A last-minute social invitation? Great, go for it. Start a new leisure activity? Why not. This may be your cue to spend less time glued to your schedule and more time participating in life.

Virgo is your travel sector and Virgo season – 22 August to 22 September – is an ideal time for you to go on holiday every year. Plus, this year, there are not one but two New Moons in Virgo and this is unusual.

A New Moon is a symbol of new beginnings and a time to be proactive and take the initiative. The first New Moon takes place on 23 August, a great date to set off on holiday or set new intentions around future trips, adventures and life-changing experiences.

The second New Moon is a solar eclipse in Virgo on 21

September, the day before the equinox. A solar eclipse is a turbo-powered New Moon, a time when the unexpected may kick in. There might be a twist of fate linked to this eclipse that brings a new experience your way. You could become an author, step into a new research role or be invited on the trip of a lifetime.

If a new opportunity comes to light which enables you to use your expertise and pass on what you know, say yes. Use the earth sign energy in your life to embrace new experiences and maximise the potential of your personal skills, gifts and talents.

RULING PLANET

Your traditional ruling planet is Saturn, which governs systems and organisation, order and authority. The flip side of Saturn represents restriction and limitation, fear and doubt. The plus side of Saturn represents self-discipline, commitment, hard work and long-term goals.

Saturn is in Pisces as the year begins and this is when you have some powerful conjunctions taking place. This is when you will feel Saturn's energy most strongly. Here's the pattern:

Venus conjunct Saturn Pisces –19 January

Mercury conjunct Saturn Pisces – 25 February

Sun conjunct Saturn Pisces – 12 March

Venus retrograde conjunct Saturn Pisces – 7 April

Venus conjunct Saturn Pisces – 25 April

Also, note when your ruling planet turns direct and retrograde:

Saturn turns retrograde in Aries on 13 July

Saturn turns direct in Pisces on 28 November

Finally, the dates when Saturn changes star sign are worth taking note of. Saturn enters Aries on 25 May and retreats back into Pisces on 1 September. You have all the key information explaining what this means for you in this chapter.

LUCKY DATES

Saturn Pisces sextile Uranus Taurus – 4 April

Venus enters Taurus – 6 June

Sun conjunct Jupiter Cancer – 24 June

Your Full Moon Capricorn – achievement/culmination – 10 July

Mercury turns direct in Leo – 11 August

Mars enters Capricorn – 15 December

Venus enters Capricorn – 24 December

There are no New Moons in Capricorn this year. The last one fell on 30 December 2024. The next one will fall on 18 January 2026.

AQUARIUS

YOUR 2025 HOROSCOPE

AQUARIUS RULERSHIPS

ZODIAC SYMBOL: THE WATER BEARER

RULING PLANET: TRADITIONAL –
SATURN, GOD OF ORGANISATION;
MODERN – URANUS, GOD OF INVENTION

MODE/ELEMENT: FIXED AIR –
HUMANITARIAN, STRUCTURED,
COLLECTIVE GOALS, PRINCIPLED

COLOUR: ELECTRIC BLUE, NEON COLOURS

ARCHETYPE: THE SCIENTIST, THE HIPPY

YOUR TOP TIPS FOR 2025

MAKE MONEY FROM GAMING,
PURSUE A HOBBY AVIDLY

DO WORK THAT'S MEANINGFUL,
CHAMPION YOUR COLLEAGUES

STEP INTO A SPEAKING ROLE,
LEAD A PROTEST

CLEAN UP YOUR FINANCES,
FIND YOUR MONEY FLOW

TRANSFORM YOUR PERSONAL LIFE
AND YOUR RELATIONSHIPS

PLAY TIME

Jupiter is the planet of joy and good fortune. Therefore, wherever Jupiter goes in your horoscope is where you're likely to find happiness, expansion and growth. Jupiter entered your fellow air sign Gemini on 25 May 2024 where it will remain until 9 June. This could feel like a breath of fresh air. Turn your focus to what you want out of life. This is because Gemini rules creativity, entertainment, fun, children and romance. It's the playful sector of your horoscope and it's about doing more of what you love. This includes games, hobbies and anything you enjoy outside of work. When Jupiter's in Gemini, it's an ideal time to embrace your passion and desire. Plan fun events with friends and family and make entertainment, laughter and socialising high priority. Focus on the positives and steer away from negative vibes.

Being a Sun Aquarius, you are one of the social air signs and you often have a diverse circle of friends. Plus, Gemini is the star sign of communication. Therefore, Jupiter in Gemini is ideal for social events, making introductions and bringing people together. You could start a singles night, take up bingo or join your local public speaking group. Whatever appeals to you personally.

Jupiter is the planet of luck too, so trust your luck and have a flutter, enter a competition or buy a raffle ticket when you're out and about. There's a popular saying in the UK: 'you have to be in to win'. This can apply to life as well as the lottery; e.g. if you want to meet someone new, join a dating agency or let your friends know you're keen for an introduction. This will work better than sitting home alone waiting for the phone to ring. It's a similar scenario if you've always wanted to launch a radio programme, draw cartoons or become a stand-up comic. Get out there and make it happen.

While Jupiter's in Gemini, revisit your childhood dreams. Hang out with children and let their delight and joy in life rub off on you.

There are some lucky dates when Jupiter's in Gemini. Firstly, the Sun and talk planet Mercury are in your star sign and team up with Jupiter on 30 January and 3 February. You could line up something special on or around these dates linked to your personal goals or aims. Plan something fun, reach out and make connections.

Fast forward to 6 April, 5 May and 5 June, and the inner planets are moving through Aries and your communication and community sector. On these dates, they align with lucky Jupiter, which is great for group events and extending your social circle. You might be organising a village fete or charity event. Alternatively, you could be joining in with a protest or group demonstration.

Your communication sector is ruled by Aries, a star sign that knows how to put anger to good effect, so be assertive and take the lead. Be fuelled by your passion and tap into the humanitarian side of your Aquarius nature. Your star sign is linked to the collective and you're at your best when you're playing an active role within society.

The stand-out date while Jupiter is in Gemini is 8 June. This is when there's a Mercury–Jupiter conjunction in your creativity sector. As both Mercury and Jupiter are linked to education, this would be a wonderful time to take a test or exam linked to a hobby or interest. It's a social combination. Yet, mastery is a key theme running through your horoscope this year and Gemini rules your skills, gifts and talents. Be social but pursue your interests and leisure activities too, the things in life that give you pleasure. This is about doing more of what you love, for pleasure's sake.

Jupiter's good fortune could come your way while Jupiter is in Gemini. Alternatively, you might be proud of a child's success. Encourage your children to talk and step back from phones and social media. Arrange social events with them. Alternatively, if your children live far away, put a regular phone call in place.

There's another important reason why you're wise to focus on these key areas of your life moving forward. This is because your modern ruling planet, Uranus, will be in Gemini from 7 July to 8 November. Uranus returns to Gemini next year on 26 April 2026, where it remains for the following seven years. Uranus is one of the slower-moving generational planets and doesn't change star sign very often. Therefore, the fact that Uranus is moving into Gemini and your creativity sector is big news.

Gemini rules the things in life that you 'give birth to', including children and creative projects. Uranus is the innovator and awakener and its nature is spontaneous and quick. Uranus is linked to technology and, if you're a typical Aquarius, you'll use technology to your advantage.

Yet Uranus in Gemini is urging you to say yes to play and pleasure, the things in life you love the most. This might include children or a niche hobby or interest.

Events on or around 12 August and 29 August could point the way forward. This is when Uranus in Gemini teams up with planets in Aries and your communication sector. On 12 August, Uranus teams up with Saturn, which means you have your two ruling planets working together. This feels powerful, perhaps presenting an opportunity where you can turn something old into something new. This is because Saturn represents experience and knowledge and gives a nod to the past. Whereas Uranus represents innovation and future ideas. You may be able to develop your work or a personal project in a new and progressive way.

Take what you already know or have experienced and repurpose it as something new and different. It's not necessarily about starting over completely. It's about bringing your proven skills into the new age, in a way that's innovative and unique. Start a blog or newsletter and let your creativity run through you. Whether your thing is quantum physics, tattoo art, breath work, parachute jumping or engineering, embrace your passion fully and share it with the world.

WORK AND HEALTH

On 9 June, the planet of opportunity, Jupiter, enters water sign Cancer, where it remains until 30 June 2026. Cancer rules your work and routine, your lifestyle and health. It's about the basics of life and your everyday well-being. This isn't necessarily about working harder; it's about bringing more joy into your work and routine and aiming for a healthy work/life balance.

Cancer is an emotional water sign, encouraging you to tap into your intuition and do what feels right, rather than what you think is right. If you're not in the right job, or you're doing work that you find stressful or boring, this may be harder to continue once Jupiter's in Cancer. This combination favours flow in life, less stress and more comfort.

While Jupiter's moving through Cancer, you may find the ideal job that frees up your time or fall in love with volunteering. Cancer's nature is caring and kind, and emotional connections matter. When you're doing something helpful for other people, this brings you emotional fulfilment in return. There's less focus on status and ambition and more focus on work that makes a difference and matters to other people or your community. You could get involved with your local union while Jupiter's moving through Cancer or become an advocate of employees' rights. Perhaps you move into a customer service or government role. Or you use your hallmark Aquarius traits of social conscience and ethics to be of service in a way that suits you.

Good health is part of Jupiter's journey through Cancer. Be aware of the mind-body-spirit connection and make healthy choices regarding your lifestyle and well-being. When it comes to exercise, find your thing. You might start circuit training, learn tai chi or take up tango. Or perhaps you're into cycling, whether you have a goal to enter the Tour de France or you're putting in the miles on your spin bike.

When you have more energy physically, this tips over into your working life and routine and is good for your mental health. You'll find you can get more done. The dates when this activity peaks are 24 June and 12 August. This is when there's a lucky Sun–Jupiter conjunction in Cancer, on 24 June, and an abundant Venus–Jupiter conjunction in Cancer, on 12 August. These combinations promise good fortune. Look out for new opportunities which come your way. This could be a new work opportunity or volunteering role. Or something that's linked to your health and well-being. You might find the perfect health practitioner or get the correct diagnosis for an ongoing ailment.

On 22 June, 12 September and 8 October, Jupiter in Cancer connects with planets in Virgo and your joint finance sector. These would be positive dates to sign a contract or start a savings plan. The theme is security and getting things organised, regarding your home or family.

Later in the year, the star sign Scorpio is prominent – this rules your career and vocation. Action planet Mars is here from 22 September to 4 November, and you may sense your ambitions rising.

Jupiter teams up with the inner planets in Scorpio on 24 October, 28 October, 17 November, 26 November and 6 December. Anything that begins under Jupiter's gaze promises success. Be expansive during this period and aim to grow your business or expand your connections. This peak astrology could coincide with the start of a new job. Yet, whatever you begin is potentially life-changing and transformative.

There is one proviso, however, because Mercury is retrograde from 9 November to 29 November. This is a time to take your foot off the accelerator and slow things down. Avoid making any major work or health decision until Mercury's back to direct motion. This is when new information often comes to light.

Also, as the year begins, you may not be feeling optimistic about your work or health. This is because action planet Mars is retrograde in Cancer from 6 January to 24 February. Sometimes, this is a period when you're unemployed. Or you have to rethink or review your work situation and lifestyle. Try not to become overly frustrated if things aren't working out.

Once Mars is moving direct in Cancer from 24 February to

18 April, you may find it easier to get things done. Mars is a physical planet, encouraging you to get fit and work hard.

When Jupiter is in Cancer later in the year, this is an easier influence. The more you're in flow and in step with the rhythm of life and the universe, the more you will find that new opportunities open up for you. Tune into your emotional intelligence and intuit your way forward.

WORDS AND IDEOLOGIES

Your traditional planet is Saturn, adding a serious note to your character. Saturn is the academic and scientist, the planet linked to systems, rules and boundaries. This year, Saturn is changing star sign, which is always an important shift for you. On 25 May, Saturn enters Aries, where it will remain until 1 September. Saturn returns to Aries on 14 February 2026 until April 2028.

This adds clout and authority to your communication sector, whether you step up your game or you find a vehicle for your voice. Aries rules the written and spoken word in your horoscope. It's about your place within the community and represents the sharing of knowledge, networks and ideas. This is about education and gaining qualifications, a time to take yourself seriously. Perhaps you add letters to your name or gain new qualifications. You might decide to go back to school and improve your knowledge or further your credentials. Saturn rules commitment and discipline. Therefore, it's a promising period to sign up to a two- or three-year course. Or to step into a teaching role and pass on your knowledge.

Saturn in Aries is a strong symbol for public speaking and becoming a voice of authority. This may coincide with you taking on a significant role in your community or your neighbourhood. Aries rules your siblings and close relatives too.

You may already be on a new journey of learning or education. This is because of the recent eclipse cycle cutting across the Aries/Libra axis of the zodiac. This began in March 2023 and completes in March 2025.

You may have been able to combine study with travel over the last couple of years. Perhaps your interests and experiences have attracted attention from abroad or global connections, or you've enjoyed combining the two areas on a holiday study course.

This year, there's a powerful New Moon solar eclipse in Aries on 29 March. A solar eclipse is a New Moon with turbo power behind it, when the wheel of fortune turns, signposting a new path ahead. Sometimes, one door has to close before a new door opens during an eclipse. Bear this symbolism in mind.

Yet, it's an invitation to step up your game. You could be asked to talk at a major event or be on stage for a conference or workshop. Perhaps you're invited for an interview or podcast collaboration. Your stars are encouraging you to be seen and heard.

There's a lot of planetary activity in Aries and your communication sector early in the year. This is because of what's happening with the social planets Venus and Mercury. Venus is in Aries from 4 February to 27 March, and again from 30 April to 6 June. Mercury is in Aries from 3 March to 30 March, and again from 16 April to 10 May. This suggests that there's a lot happening within your community or your local neighbourhood. Alternatively, you might be involved with a new group of people online. You may be learning a language or start a youth group. You might be enjoying the power of words or be teaching English to foreign speakers. Or perhaps you're simply keen to share ideas and make new friends. Reach out to other people and extend your network early in the year.

Also this year, one of the slower-moving generational planets Neptune enters Aries. Neptune will be in Aries from 30 March to 22 October, and returns to Aries on 26 January 2026 until 2038/2039. Neptune represents fantasy and the imagination, which conjures up the beauty of words. It's an ideological influence and, alongside Saturn, this combination feels political.

Saturn and Neptune are side by side in June, July and August. This is in preparation for their epic conjunction in Aries in February 2026, the first time these two planets will come together since 1989. Your social conscience is likely to be strong during this period. Notice who or what triggers your moral compass and stand firm on your beliefs.

Saturn provides the anchor to keep you grounded but use Neptune's influence to push back the boundaries of life. This combination could see you seeking a spiritual path, or perhaps you lose yourself in the wonder of film and images. You might be making a documentary or be a budding film-maker.

Together, Saturn and Neptune can help turn dreams into reality. Yet, be wary of allowing your thoughts and words to become negative. Use this combination to find solace and comfort in words, community and communication.

There is one period in the year when it may be wise to take a step back from fighting your corner – from 15 June to 19 June, when Jupiter in Cancer clashes with Saturn and Neptune. Be wary of speaking out during these few days, if this could damage your reputation or harm your position at work.

MONEY FLOW

Your planet, Saturn, starts its journey out of Pisces this year, where it's been since March 2023. Pisces is the star sign which rules money, assets and possessions in your horoscope. Wherever Saturn goes, you have to work hard and be sensible. Perhaps you've been saving money or you've been through a period of hardship. Saturn remains in Pisces until 25 May. It returns from 1 September to 14 February 2026, but then it's gone for the next thirty years.

As the year begins, you're wise to be thinking about money and decide what's important moving forward. If you're in a place where you can't see the end of financial difficulty, know that Saturn is a slow-moving planet. It's about building for the future. Use the timing of Saturn to aim to bring an end to any financial challenge and to get your finances straight.

Also this year, Neptune is completing its journey through Pisces. Neptune leaves Pisces on 30 March and is back from 22 October to 26 January 2026. Neptune has been in your money sector since 2012 and this can play out in different ways. Sometimes, finances feel boundless when Neptune's here. You're in tune with the flow of the universe. When you have trust and faith in life, money comes your way when you need it. It's not a grasping or materialistic influence. In fact, it's the opposite. Wherever Neptune goes, it's encouraging you to surrender to life and to trust in a divine force to protect you.

The flip side of Neptune is seduction and betrayal, which can play out as being scammed. Pisces' activity is in flow in the first few months of the year, so work with Neptune in a way that benefits you.

Saturn and Neptune together are encouraging you to manifest

a financial goal. This would be a good combination for running a charity or fundraising.

Early in the year, the planet of communication, Mercury, and the planet of love and money, Venus, are both active in Pisces. This favours discussions around money and working alongside other people to boost your finances. There may be a link between money and love.

However, be aware that both planets will be retrograde in March and April. Venus is retrograde from 2 March to 13 April, and Mercury is retrograde from 15 March to 7 April. This is not the time to make a major investment. Put your foot on the brake and spend less, not more. Sometimes, new information or a better deal comes to light once the planets are back to direct motion.

There is another influence involving the North Node, which moves into Pisces on 12 January. This is where it remains until 26 July 2026. The nodes are linked to the path of destiny. Trust in the signs and synchronicities which come your way. This is opposite to your Aquarius nature, which is logical and uses the power of the mind to make sense of things. Experiment with tapping into something deeper that takes you beyond rational explanation.

The nodes follow the eclipses and, in 2025, you're in the midst of a powerful eclipse cutting across the Virgo/Pisces axis of the zodiac and the financial sectors of your horoscope. Wherever the eclipses fall, life tends to more unstable as unexpected events and drama kicks in. You can win big but potentially lose big.

This eclipse cycle began in September 2024 and completes in February 2027. This year, there are two Full Moon lunar eclipses, one in Virgo on 14 March and one in Pisces on 7 September.

Things can emerge during an eclipse that have been hidden. Sometimes, lunar eclipse symbolism reveals who you're up against and there can be a theme of competition. Ideally, you want to end up on the winning team.

Eclipses are notoriously shadowy, so get your financial ducks in a row before eclipse season kicks in.

Also this year, there are two New Moons in Virgo, your joint finance sector, and this is unusual. The first takes place on 23 August and is an ideal date to sign a contract or agree a financial deal. The second New Moon is a solar eclipse in Virgo on 21 September. A solar eclipse is a New Moon with extra oomph. Things can happen quickly and it accelerates growth. It may be that more courage is required in financial affairs.

You're being asked to step up your game regarding money and finances this year. Do whatever's necessary to secure your financial future and be cash savvy. Aim to tap into a different way of doing things and find your money flow.

A NEW DIRECTION

We are moving into a new air sign era. And, as you're one of the air signs, this suggests that you may be one of the movers and shakers of the new era.

This year, power planet Pluto is established in your star sign, where it's going to remain for the next twenty years. Pluto moved in and out of Aquarius in 2023/2024. This is powerful for you and may coincide with a new direction in life. Aquarius is your personal sector linked to your goals and aims, your image and profile. It's how you see the world and how the world sees you.

Aquarius is the star sign linked to the collective and, theoretically, Pluto here gives power to the people. This shift could be major out in the world over the next twenty years and it's significant for you. You're likely to know what this is about in your birthday month, Aquarius season, which runs from 19 January to 18 February.

Pluto teams up with the Sun on 21 January and talk planet Mercury on 29 January. At its best, Pluto can be an empowering force, urging you to step up your game. There is also a theme of the survivor around Pluto. Sometimes it's when you experience life's challenges or the dark side of life that you become stronger. Pluto can be a ruthless influence and a time when you're wise to dig deep and 'know thyself'. This can be a powerful period of self-transformation.

Also this year, your co-ruler Uranus changes star sign. Since 2018, Uranus has been at the base of your horoscope in the star sign Taurus. Taurus rules your home and family, also your past, your roots, your legacy and where you come from.

Uranus here can feel rootless or unsettling. As Uranus moves through Taurus until 7 July, consider what might be changing in the foundations of your life. Uranus returns to Taurus on 8 November but will be gone for the next eighty years on 26 April 2026. There's an endgame theme to Uranus as it moves in and out of Taurus. You may be ready to move on, to leave the past behind and start afresh.

Also, Uranus in Taurus connects with your co-ruler Saturn in Pisces on 4 April. This links home and family with finances, your values and self-worth. What are you ready to pursue in your life that may give you more freedom or flexibility?

Things could speed up towards the end of this year. Scorpio is the star sign opposite Taurus, at the peak of your horoscope.

Scorpio represents your future path, linked to your career and vocation, your public profile.

Action planet Mars is powering through Scorpio from 22 September to 4 November. Talk planet Mercury is here twice, from 6 October to 29 October, and again from 19 November to 11 December. Plus, this is Scorpio season, when the Sun is in Scorpio from 23 October to 22 November. Put all this together and it's potentially an ambitious time of year, when you might step into a position of power or influence.

Mercury is retrograde from 9 November to 29 November, so avoid making the big decisions then. However, there is a theme of past connections while Mercury's in retreat. For example, it's a good time to reach out to past employers.

During this period, Uranus opposes the planets in Scorpio on 19 November, 21 November, 30 November and 6 December. This feels unpredictable and could bring the unexpected. Perhaps, you have to move home because of a new job. Or events at home or within your family are the reason why you're stepping into a new role or adjusting your life path.

Yet, if the wheel of fortune is calling you this year, asking you to step up your game and embrace a new direction – you're wise to say yes.

LOVE LIFE

If you're a typical Aquarius, you often lead an unconventional love life, thanks to your co-ruler Uranus. For example, a younger partner, an open marriage or a preference for dating rather than commitment. Basically, you like to do whatever's right for you. Your personal relationships enter a new phase this year, and it's one that's exciting, dramatic and ripe for change.

Firstly, live-wire Uranus enters air sign Gemini on 7 July. Gemini rules romance and love affairs in your horoscope and Uranus remains here until 8 November. This promises spontaneity when it comes to love. If you're single, events could take a sudden turn when Uranus lights up your romance sector. This might awaken something inside you. Or perhaps you encounter an unusual individual who bursts into your life. This can mean you fall for someone who's older or younger. Or someone who's not your usual type.

If you're married or in a long-term relationship, it's a cosmic reminder to spice up your love life, including your sex life. Don't take love for granted when Uranus is causing a revolution in your romance sector. Recreate date nights, start a new hobby together or relive your youth.

Gemini rules children and pregnancy in your horoscope, and events could happen quickly. Ensure you practise safe sex if you're not ready to become a parent. Otherwise, expect the unexpected and know that your kids are going to keep you on your toes!

Your relationships have been caught up in a stop-start scenario for some time now. Since the middle of 2023, the inner planets Venus, Mars and Mercury have all spent some time retrograde in Leo and your relationship sector. Perhaps a relationship has been on and off for some time or you've spent time away from your partner, for whatever reason.

As 2025 begins, passion planet Mars is retrograde in Leo until 6 January. It turned retrograde here on 6 December 2024. This is encouraging you to focus on love and your one to ones immediately the year begins.

As the planets move in and out of Leo, they encounter Pluto in Aquarius. These can be challenging oppositions and the key dates are 3 January, 27 April, 29 June and 25 July. A relationship could come to an end under these stars. Or perhaps you're the one who's changing and, therefore, seeing love differently. The balance of power may be out in a love relationship. Or you want to move away from a partnership that's become controlling.

Talk planet Mercury will be in Leo for an unusually long time, from 26 June to 2 September. This is where Mercury turns retrograde, from 18 July to 11 August. This is when you're wise to slow things down, take a step back and give yourself time and space to decide what you want moving forward.

Relationships are a hot spot for you this year. The good news is that there's plenty of forward-moving action in Leo and your relationship sector. Mars is moving forward in Leo from 18 April to 17 June. The Sun is in Leo from 22 July to 22 August. And the planet of love, Venus, is in Leo from 25 August to 19 September. It's a busy sector of your horoscope. One way or another, life is calling you to engage actively with your relationships and decide what you want when it comes to love.

This is potentially a year of transformation for you, which will no doubt impact your love life. Or perhaps it's meeting someone new, which is the catalyst for change.

RULING PLANETS

You are one of only three star signs that has two ruling planets. Your traditional ruler is Saturn, ruling systems and organisation, order and authority. When Uranus was discovered in 1781, it became your modern ruling planet. Uranus represents change, the modern world, technology, innovation and rebellion. Saturn plays by the rules whereas Uranus likes to break them. You may recognise different aspects of your nature in these two key archetypes.

Saturn and Uranus are slower moving planets so it's important to note when they make key conjunctions with the inner planets. This is when you feel their energy most strongly. This takes place for Saturn when it's completing its journey through Pisces, and for Uranus when it's completing its journey through Taurus. Here's the pattern:

Venus conjunct Saturn Pisces – 19 January

Mercury conjunct Saturn Pisces – 25 February

Sun conjunct Saturn Pisces – 12 March

Venus retrograde conjunct Saturn Pisces – 7 April

Venus conjunct Saturn Pisces – 25 April

Sun conjunct Uranus Taurus – 17 May

Mercury conjunct Uranus Taurus – 24 May

Venus conjunct Uranus Taurus – 4 July

Also, note when your ruling planets turn direct and retrograde. This is because a planet's energy is often more intense when it switches direction. Here's the pattern:

Saturn turns retrograde in Aries – 13 July; Saturn turns direct in Pisces – 28 November

Uranus turns direct in Taurus – 30 January; Uranus turns retrograde in Gemini – 6 September

Finally, the dates when Saturn and Uranus change star signs are worth taking note of. Saturn enters Aries on 25 May and retreats back into Pisces on 1 September. Uranus enters Gemini on 7 July and retreats back into Taurus on 8 November.

You have all the information explaining what these events mean for you in this section.

LUCKY DATES

Your New Moon Aquarius – new beginnings – 29 January

Sun Aquarius trine Jupiter Gemini – 30 January

Mercury Aquarius trine Jupiter Gemini – 3 February

Mercury conjunct Jupiter Gemini – 8 June

Venus conjunct Uranus Taurus – 4 July

Uranus enters Gemini – 7 July

Your Full Moon Aquarius – achievement/culmination – 9 August

Saturn Aries sextile Uranus Gemini – 12 August

PISCES

YOUR 2025 HOROSCOPE

PISCES RULERSHIPS

ZODIAC SYMBOL: TWO FISH
SWIMMING IN OPPOSITE DIRECTIONS

RULING PLANET: TRADITIONAL –
JUPITER, GOD OF EXPANSION; MODERN –
NEPTUNE, GOD OF THE SEA

MODE/ELEMENT: MUTABLE WATER –
SENTIMENTAL, REFLECTIVE, CARING,
IMAGINATIVE

COLOUR: SEA GREEN; BLUE; AQUAMARINE

ARCHETYPE: THE DREAMER, THE MYSTIC

TOP TIPS FOR 2025

BUY A CAMPERVAN,
EXPAND YOUR FAMILY

LET YOUR INNER CREATIVE
OR ARTIST OUT TO PLAY

LEAD A MINIMALIST LIFESTYLE,
START A SAVINGS PLAN

DISCOVER YOUR CALLING, PURSUE
A HEALING OR SPIRITUAL PATH

GET MARRIED, SAY YES TO LOVE

HOME AND FAMILY

Jupiter is your traditional ruling planet, the planet of luck and opportunity. Wherever Jupiter goes, it's worth following. When you make the most of Jupiter in your life, you can chase your dreams and go after the things in life that make you happy.

In 2025, the cosmic spotlight turns towards the foundations of your horoscope as Jupiter is in Gemini. Gemini rules your home and family, your past and your roots. Jupiter entered Gemini on 25 May 2024, where it will remain until 9 June. This is a classic time to move home or expand where you live.

Jupiter rules foreign connections too. Therefore, you may be planning a move abroad or a get-together with family who live around the world or in different parts of the country.

Like your star sign Pisces, Gemini is one of the mutable star signs, which means you like to be flexible and you need variety in life. Gemini's zodiac symbol is the twins. The ideal scenario with Jupiter in Gemini might be to have two homes or be able to spend time in the city and by the sea. Consider how you might be able to bring more flexibility into your living situation.

Jupiter is the planet linked to joy, so a big family celebration would be well-starred during the first half of the year. It's the perfect time to catch up with people from your past, to remember your roots and where you come from. You might be working on your family tree, be writing your memoirs or be involved in recording the memories of your past. This is because Gemini is the communication star sign and wants to give a voice to your past and your legacy. Or this could be a time when you're expanding your family, whether this involves your children, the addition of a step family or opening your doors to other people.

If you're a typical Sun Pisces, your nature is to care for others. You often take on a role of looking after vulnerable people or adopting stray animals.

On 30 January and 3 February, Jupiter connects with planets in Aquarius and the hidden sector of your horoscope. You may take a trip down memory lane or the past catches up with you in some way. You may discover secrets or memories via the internet, as Aquarius is the star sign linked to technology. Or you're using modern techniques to preserve past experiences.

Fast forward to 6 April, 5 May and 5 June, and the inner planets in Aries and your personal money sector link to Jupiter in Gemini. These would be ideal dates to invest in property, spend money on your home or finance a child's education. Be wary of the first date, however, when two planets are retrograde. Notice what new opportunities come in but ideally delay taking action until mid-April.

The stand-out date for home and family affairs is arguably 8 June, when there's a Mercury–Jupiter conjunction in your home and family sector. Mercury is the communication planet, so this could coincide with good news or a family celebration. It's a social and educational combination too, so perhaps, you decide to home school. Or you're making some big decisions about your family's education.

Jupiter works in synchronous ways and it's important to put

yourself in its path. Say yes to a new home or family opportunity that comes your way while Jupiter is in Gemini. Think of these key areas of your life as a place of growth and expansion.

Jupiter leaves Gemini in June but another major planet enters Gemini on 7 July. That planet is Uranus, linked to independence and change. Uranus remains in Gemini until 8 November. Then, it returns to Gemini on 26 April 2026, where it will be for the following seven years. This could indicate a new chapter in your life, which will be more unconventional regarding your home and family. You might feel less attached to the past as your gaze turns towards the future. Perhaps, you want to move out of your comfort zone and shake up your current situation. Or other people moving in or out of your home could leave you feeling unsettled or rootless. Or perhaps you recognise it's time to move on and embrace a more independent or freedom-loving lifestyle. While Uranus is in Gemini, you could buy a campervan and decide to hit the road at the weekends and on your time off. Or you could be entering a nomadic phase, when you're less interested in possessions and are yearning for a freer lifestyle.

Events in August could prove pivotal, when Uranus teams up with Saturn and your co-ruler Neptune in Aries, your personal money sector. The key dates are 12 August and 29 August. Whatever you're planning that's new and different, this would be a great month to set off in search of a different lifestyle.

CREATIVITY AND FUN

Jupiter in Gemini is speedy and quick. You may be juggling a lot of different balls or spend a lot of time dealing with home and family affairs in the first half of the year. Therefore, it may come as something of a relief when Jupiter enters your fellow water sign Cancer on 9 June. Jupiter will remain here until 30 June 2026.

In your horoscope, the water signs are where the focus turns towards you and what brings you pleasure. When Jupiter moves into Cancer, you may realise that the balance of life is out and you've been prioritising other people. If so, this is the time to put yourself and your interests first. Cancer rules creativity, romance, entertainment, fun and children in your horoscope. It's the playful sector and it's about doing more of what you love. Here's your opportunity to embrace your passion and follow your desires.

Being a Sun Pisces, you are one of the most creative of the star signs and your modern ruler, Neptune, is linked to film, images and dreams. Somewhere in life, you need a place where you can lose yourself, in a good way. One of the easiest ways to escape the mundane and everyday side of life is to pursue a creative or artistic passion. Pisces is linked to music, film, poetry, art – wherever in life you find your creative muse. While Jupiter's in Cancer, here's your opportunity to devote yourself to your art. Perhaps you take up film studies, attend your local open mic night or have a creative day once a week. Bring more music, art, poetry and soul into your life.

There's strong emphasis here as soon as Jupiter enters Cancer. On 24 June, there's a lucky Sun–Jupiter conjunction in Cancer. Then, on 12 August, there's a lovely Venus–Jupiter conjunction in Cancer. These would be wonderful dates to pursue pleasure or grab your five minutes of fame. When you actively engage with your natural skills and talents, and do more of what you love, this boosts your self-confidence and brings more joy into your world.

Plus, this sector of your horoscope is linked to luck. It's your planet Jupiter which is a reminder that luck is an attitude. When you have a vision in life, a willingness to take a leap of faith and believe in yourself, you attract luck and good fortune to you. Think of yourself as lucky and see what materialises. Buy a raffle ticket or enter a talent competition, whatever works for you personally.

Later in the year, Jupiter is in action when it teams up with planets in Scorpio and your travel and study sector. The key dates are 24 October, 28 October, 17 November, 22 November, 26 November and 6 December. This would be a wonderful time to book a holiday or sign up for an educational course. Wherever you feel called to pursue a new path in life, go for it. You might be exploring philosophy, the mysteries of life or a new religion.

Communication planet Mercury is retrograde from 9 November to 29 November. This would be a positive few weeks to immerse yourself in a study project or go on retreat. Take your foot off the accelerator of life and pursue an activity that's meaningful as well as fun and joyful.

As the year begins, however, you may feel thwarted in your attempts to bring more pleasure into your life. This is because action planet Mars is retrograde in Cancer from 6 January to 24 February. Sometimes, when Mars is in retreat, things don't work out. Or you don't have the energy, willpower or motivation to chase after the things you want in life. Be patient and, at the very least, set some New Year's resolutions to pursue more play and pleasure in life, as the year progresses.

Cancer rules children in your horoscope too. In fact, it represents all the things in life that you 'give birth to'. You may spend more time with children, either your own or other people's. Children are often a wonderful reminder to experience joy, to laugh and be playful.

As Jupiter expands what it touches, this is a nod towards expanding your own family. Cancer is a fertile star sign ruled by the nurturing Moon. What will you give birth to in 2025? Will it be a child, a work of art or a creative masterpiece?

MONEY AND VALUES

Saturn is the planet of authority and responsibility, and this year, Saturn changes star sign. This is an important shift as Saturn remains in each star sign of the zodiac for two to three years. From 25 May to 1 September, Saturn will be in Aries, the star sign which rules your money, assets and possessions. Saturn returns to Aries next year on 14 February 2026 until April 2028.

When Saturn's in Aries, you're wise to pay close attention to your finances. Decide where you need to be committed or sensible around money. Saturn favours a long-term steady plan rather than attempting to boost your fortunes overnight. Plus, Saturn's nature is to save rather than spend. While Saturn's in Aries, you could start a savings plan or consider where you can invest your money wisely. This might be a time when you decide to adopt a minimalist lifestyle, cut back on expenses or live more frugally. Alternatively, you might be on a mission to work hard and earn money. Perhaps, you have some key financial goals that you're working towards.

Aries not only rules your personal money, but also your values and self-esteem. Therefore, it's important not to diminish your sense of self-worth while Saturn's in Aries. Keep believing in yourself and ensure your financial dealings reflect your values. Don't undermine yourself and stand firm to ensure you get paid what you deserve.

At best, Saturn can be a steadying influence. Perhaps this is what's needed, as you've recently experienced a lively eclipse cycle, cutting across the Aries/Libra axis of the zodiac and the financial sectors of your horoscope. This eclipse cycle began in March 2023 and completes in March 2025. Eclipses often coincide with the highs and lows of life. They can symbolise accelerated growth, though also drama or crisis.

The last eclipse in this cycle takes place on 29 March and it's a New Moon solar eclipse in Aries. A solar eclipse is a New Moon with extra oomph. It's turbo-powered and things can happen fast. What's important to note is that Aries represents your personal money. Therefore, it's wise to be self-centred and assertive when it comes to money and prioritise your own interests. Consider what this might mean for you.

During the eclipse, however, there's a double whammy of retrograde planets. Talk planet Mercury is retrograde from 15 March to 7 April, and the planet of relating, Venus, is retrograde from 2 March to 13 April. Plus, both planets spend an unusually long time in Aries and your money sector in the first few months of the year. This suggests that there may be a lot to negotiate and discuss around money. Notice in particular where love and money are linked.

You might be playing a waiting game if you're due money during the retrograde phase. And it's not a time to make a major investment. Also, Venus represents money and Mercury is linked to the money markets. Both retrograde phases often coincide with a topsy-turvy time for finances. Keep close tabs on what's happening and see if you can take advantage of a shifting situation. Keep talking, keep negotiating, but wait to make any important financial decision until mid-April. This is when more information may come to light, as Mercury turns direct on 7 April followed by Venus on 13 April.

Finances are likely to be a significant part of your life for some years to come. This is because another major planet changes star sign. Your modern ruler, Neptune, enters Aries on 30 March, where it will remain until 22 October. Neptune returns to Aries on 26 January 2026 until 2038/2039. Neptune is the planet of dreams and the imagination, linked to fantasy rather than reality. You may have big financial dreams, yet you need an additional planet that can act both as an anchor and as a reality check.

This year, you find that in the shape of Saturn. Saturn and Neptune are side by side in Aries in June, July and August, preparing for their epic conjunction here in February 2026. When both planets are working together, you can turn your dreams into reality. Plus, there's a charitable, giving side to Neptune. Therefore, if you're wealthy, you may want to give your money away and step into a new role as philanthropist. You could develop a strong social conscience moving forward.

Neptune teaches you to surrender in life. In your finance sector, this could mean letting go of assets and material values or developing a spiritual approach to money and finances. Alternatively, it could mean putting your trust and faith in life, that it will provide for you. As a Sun Pisces, this may be something you do naturally, trusting your intuition so you can be in flow, in step with the universe.

You have a new opportunity this year to experiment with money and do things differently. Be wary, however, of letting guilt, fear or doubt kick in. There can be a negative side to Saturn and Neptune. Be alert to scams and get-rich-quick schemes.

This year's astrology doesn't suggest playing big financially. Yet, there may be some important lessons to learn around money and values.

BE MORE PISCES

Saturn and your co-ruler, Neptune, are starting their respective journeys out of Pisces this year. Saturn's in your star sign until 25 May and again from 1 September to 14 February 2026. Neptune's in Pisces up until 30 March and again from 22 October to 26 January 2026.

Saturn in Pisces is an unusual combination; you've had the planet of discipline and hard work in your star sign since March 2023. On the plus side, Saturn in Pisces can mean you step up your game. You become serious about your personal goals and getting things done. It can help you put firm boundaries in place, to keep yourself safe and conserve your energy. However, sometimes Saturn in your star sign slows you down or indicates a period of ill health, low energy or hardship.

Yet, Saturn doesn't only represent hard work, as this is the planet of the shaman. Saturn favours solitude and is linked to wisdom and knowledge. Therefore, perhaps you're on a journey of the spirit.

In the first few months of this year, the activity in Pisces reaches a peak. Firstly, the North Node enters Pisces on 12 January, where it will remain until 26 July 2026. This often coincides with a calling when you feel the path of destiny opening up before you. Fate steps in and leads you in a new direction.

Be true to your Pisces archetype early this year and tap into your dreams and the collective unconscious. At its purest, your star sign represents the things in life that connect you with the divine, with spirit and the interconnectedness of all things. This is a powerful time to listen to your inner voice and recognise the oneness of all things. This might make complete sense to you or perhaps it's a path you're starting to explore.

Notice what invitations or opportunities open up for you early in the year. You might find a local group who are involved in pursuing a spiritual path. Or perhaps you hear or read about meditation, yoga, energy work, shamanism, sound healing, art therapy or the wonders of the cosmos. Be alert to the signs and synchronicities that are opening up before you. Also, the social planets Venus and Mercury are active in Pisces, calling you to join in with others, to find your tribe, your group.

Venus is in Pisces from 3 January to 4 February, and again from 27 March to 30 April. Mercury is in Pisces from 14 February to 3 March, and 30 March to 16 April. This means that both planets will interact with Saturn, Neptune and the North Node in Pisces numerous times. The astrology is awash with energy and revelation in your star sign. This is a powerful time in the year when you may find yourself and discover more about your place in the universe. Or you have a calling to share your knowledge and wisdom.

Also this year, you have innovative Uranus, the awakener, in Taurus, your communication sector. Uranus has been in this sector of your horoscope since 2018 and it's starting its journey out of Taurus this year and next. Uranus is in your communication sector until 7 July and again from 8 November to 26 April 2026. Then it will be gone for another eighty years. Uranus represents the airwaves, technology and all things new and modern. It's the planet linked to groups and the collective. You could start a radio show or find a way to communicate or broadcast your ideas using technology. You might be tuning into podcasts or be listening to new and innovative programmes via the internet.

On 4 April and 20 November, Uranus in Taurus makes a powerful link to Saturn in Pisces and your co-ruler Neptune in Pisces. These dates could be significant for you, when your level of communication and personal interests are at a peak. It could be totally wacky and alternative. Perhaps you're talking with aliens, you're part of a truth group or you're meditating with a global group and tapping into higher frequencies. Or perhaps it's more prosaic and personal, like writing and sharing your poetry or doing yoga once a week.

Whatever calls you and however you identify most closely with being a Pisces, this is your year to be true to who you are.

WORK AND FUTURE PATH

You may be rethinking your work or career path as 2025 gets underway. In fact, this process may have started in the middle of 2023. This is because the retrograde phases of the inner planets Venus, Mercury and Mars have all fallen in Leo at some point since then. And Leo is one of the star signs which rules your work and routine.

These retrograde phases in Leo continue, moving into 2025. When a planet's retrograde, it turns your attention inwards. Sometimes things don't work out for you and this stops you in your tracks. Other times, you're reassessing or reviewing your situation. It can be a time of deep and personal inner change.

What you want and need starts to shift, especially when it comes to your work and lifestyle.

Action planet Mars starts the year retrograde in Leo, your work sector. Plus, almost immediately, Mars is opposed by Pluto in Aquarius on 3 January. This could signify that a job comes to an end at the start of 2025. Alternatively, you're the one who decides that you don't want to continue doing the same work or same routine moving into the year ahead.

Pluto is going to be active in Aquarius opposing planets in Leo at the start of the year, also on 27 April, 29 June and 25 July. What's coming to an end? Or where are you worn out and tired and want or need to do things differently? Pluto is the planet of power and transformation, and it moved in and out of Aquarius in 2023/2024. This year, 2025, Pluto's taken up residence here, where it remains for the next twenty years.

Aquarius is your hidden sector. It's linked to inner work, the way of the spirit and the collective consciousness. This could be a psychic and magical transit of Pluto for you, as it leads you into unexplored areas. It's taking you deeper into your psyche. You may already have an inkling what this is opening up in your life. Tap into your inner voice and trust your intuition in guiding you. Listen out for signs and synchronicities and know that the universe is always talking to you.

Pluto was god of the underworld in mythology. It's about the cycle of life, death, rebirth and renewal. You may choose to have a better relationship with death moving forward. In the Western world, we're not as comfortable with death as ancient people and people in different cultures. You could become a channeller or guide. Or, you help people transition over, on their journey between life and death. Perhaps you're gathering stories or sharing your wisdom and experiences.

Pluto moving through Aquarius could be remarkable for you, connecting you with communities on a global or wider spiritual level. This is important to note, as Pluto is opposing the inner planets moving through Leo. It may be that you go on a deep or personal journey of healing or spiritual insight, which changes your work or career and what's meaningful or possible moving forward.

Yet there is some powerful activity in your work and career sectors in 2025. Action planet Mars is strong in Leo, your work sector, from 18 April to 17 June, and in Sagittarius, your career and vocation sector, from 4 November to 15 December. These may be periods in the year when you're keen to get ahead, look for a new job or work hard at making your current job better.

Also, communication planet Mercury is going to be retrograde in these two same sectors of your horoscope and this is more of a stop-start scenario. Work with the timing of Mercury to know when to push ahead and when to put your foot on the brake. Mercury is in Leo in the middle of the year, from 26 June to 2 September. This is shining a light on your work and routine, being of service to others, your lifestyle and your health. It's no surprise that these key areas are linked in astrology. How you spend your time on a daily basis invariably impacts your health, well-being and your stress levels.

When Mercury's retrograde in Leo from 18 July to 11 August, this would be an ideal time to stop work for a while, go on holiday and chill out. Time away from your usual routine can be wonderfully creative, and also a valuable opportunity to rest and recharge your batteries.

Mercury is in Sagittarius, your career and future sector, from 29 October to 19 November, and again from 11 December onwards. Mercury's retrograde phase is from 9 November to 29

November. Therefore, line up key meetings, interviews and negotiations when Mercury's moving forward. And give yourself time in November to stop and reassess where you're heading and why.

There's a lot happening when it comes to your work and career, and timing is the key to your success. Also, you may be aware of inner rumblings that are leading you in a new direction. Listen to the calling and trust your intuition.

LOVE AND RELATIONSHIPS

It's invariably a lively time for love when you have the eclipses triggering your star sign Pisces and your relationship star sign Virgo. This is what's happening in 2025 as the current eclipse cycle continues. It began in September 2024 and will complete in February 2027.

Eclipses accelerate growth wherever they fall and things rarely remain the same. They increase the drama in your life. Therefore, you're wise to turn your attention to what you want when it comes to love and partnership, ready or not. Relationships are not an area of your life to take for granted.

This year, there are two powerful Full Moon lunar eclipses, one in Virgo on 14 March and one in Pisces on 7 September. Eclipses have a shadowy nature and often bring what's hidden to light. Sometimes, they coincide with endings and new beginnings. Relationships can be made or can be broken when an eclipse highlights the love axis of your horoscope. You may experience love more intensely too, during these powerful lunar eclipses.

Also this year, there are not one but two New Moons in

Virgo, your relationship sector, which is unusual. The first takes place on 23 August and is a symbol of a new beginning. Start afresh when it comes to love. A New Moon in Virgo spells good news for all your one-to-one collaborations. Yet, it's love that feels special and you could be planning a wedding or second honeymoon.

The second New Moon is a solar eclipse in Virgo on 21 September, the day before the equinox. A solar eclipse can coincide with a new beginning too, although sometimes one door has to close before you can start over.

Virgo rules all your one-to-one relationships, both personal and professional. It's about contracts, alliances and collaborations. It can reveal where competition lies and expose your enemies.

The wheel of fortune may turn in your direction during eclipse season and, hopefully, lead you down a positive path. Notice who comes into your life on or around the eclipse dates. This person could have a significant role to play in your life moving forward.

Also, the activity taking place in Cancer and your romance sector is important when it comes to love. Therefore, as 2025 begins, it's not a time to rush into love when passion planet Mars is retrograde in Cancer from 6 January to 24 February. Sometimes, you have a love affair when Mars is retrograde in your romance sector and it has to remain hidden. Or an ex reappears in your life. It can be a passionate period, although you're wise not to make any major decisions until Mars turns direct on 24 February.

Jupiter's move through Cancer and your romance sector can expand love. Plus, there are some key dates when Jupiter in Cancer aligns with the inner planets in Virgo, which look gorgeous for love and relationships. The key dates are 22 June,

12 September and 8 October. If you're looking for love, this could be when you meet someone new and you quickly settle into a relationship.

The stars are aligning in 2025 and suggest that this will be a big year for your relationships. Open your heart and say yes to love. It's a year when you're likely to learn more about yourself too and, possibly, at a fast rate of knots. Through your relationships and your connections with other people, your true self will be reflected back to you.

If love takes you on a big adventure this year, don't waste the opportunity to learn more about yourself at the same time. The happier you are in your own skin, the easier and more enjoyable your relationships and one to ones will become.

RULING PLANETS

You are one of only three star signs in the zodiac that has two ruling planets. Your traditional ruler is Jupiter, the best planet in astrology. Then, in 1846, when Neptune was discovered, it became your modern ruling planet.

In mythology, Jupiter was god of the sky and Neptune god of the sea. Jupiter's attributes are opportunity, expansion and growth. It's the planet linked to luck and good fortune. Neptune is the planet of dreams and the imagination, romance and fantasy. Its flip side is delusion, addiction and confusion.

Jupiter conjunctions are considered lucky dates and they're in the Lucky Dates section below. You often feel Neptune's energy most strongly when it makes conjunctions with the inner planets. This is a time when you may be more empathic or aware of your creative and spiritual source.

There are a lot of Neptune conjunctions in 2025, as both Mercury and Venus turn retrograde in your star sign. Lose yourself in a positive way and seek bliss and transcendence in your life. Here's the pattern:

Venus conjunct Neptune Pisces – 1 February

Mercury conjunct Neptune Pisces – 2 March

Sun conjunct Neptune Pisces – 19 March

Venus retrograde conjunct Neptune Pisces – 27 March

Mercury retrograde conjunct Neptune Pisces – 30 March

Mercury conjunct Neptune Aries – 17 April

Venus conjunct Neptune Aries – 2 May

Also, note when your ruling planets turn direct and retrograde. A planet's energy is more intense when it switches direction. Here's the pattern:

Jupiter turns direct in Gemini – 4 February

Jupiter turns retrograde in Cancer – 11 November

Neptune turns retrograde in Aries – 4 July

Neptune turns direct in Pisces – 10 December

Finally, the date when Jupiter changes star sign, 9 June, is worth taking note of. You have all the information explaining what this astrology means for you in this section.

LUCKY DATES

Venus conjunct North Node Pisces – 3 February

Your New Moon Pisces – new beginnings – 28 February

Venus turns direct in Pisces – 13 April

Mercury conjunct Jupiter Gemini – 8 June

Jupiter enters Cancer – 9 June

Sun conjunct Jupiter Cancer – 24 June

Venus conjunct Jupiter Cancer – 12 August

*Your Full Moon Pisces – eclipse dramas – 7 September

*Eclipses are different to normal Full Moons as your *2025 Horoscope* has described.

NEXT STEPS

If you'd like to discover more about my work as an astrologer and how this can benefit you, my website is sallykirkman.com. I write free monthly horoscopes and regular articles on the current astrology.

My most popular service is the weekly astrology newsletter subscription, which includes extensive weekly horoscopes and an easy-to-understand guide to the upcoming astrology. My subscribers love to plan their week around my astrological insight and knowledge.

I co-host my astrology podcast with my dear friend Christina Rodenbeck. It's called *Astrology Talk Podcast* and it's an hour-long show that offers you guidance on the month ahead. It's available on all major podcast platforms. We also have a selection of shorter podcasts, entitled *Astrology Talk Investigate*, in which we do just that – investigate different questions and topics through the lens of astrology.

Throughout my career, I've worked as a media astrologer and I'm often contacted by journalists to comment on current events. I was the *TV Times* astrologer for 15 years and my astrology has appeared in *Soul and Spirit* magazine, the *Daily Express*,

Prima, *Chat*, *It's Fate* and on the BBC website, to name a few. In June 2022, I was invited on to ITV's *This Morning*, talking about the link between astrology and food. And in September 2023, I taught an astrology course in Greece about making predictions using astrology.

I hope our paths will cross in the coming year and that your love of astrology will help to bring you a sense of meaning and purpose, as we continue our journey together in the wonder and chaos of life on this earth.

CONNECT WITH ME

There are many ways to connect with me and look at how we can work together. On my website, you'll find details of all my astrology services and products, including how to book an astrology reading and subscribe to my popular subscription newsletter.

On social media, my Instagram and Facebook pages are where I'm most active. Here are my social media handles, website and email address:

Website: sallykirkman.com
Email: sally@sallykirkman.com
Instagram: @sallykirkmanastrologer
Facebook: facebook.com/SallyKirkmanAstrology
Twitter: @sallykirkman
LinkedIn: linkedin.com/in/sallykirkman